A PICKLEBALL GOSPEL

The Harmony of Competition and Cooperation in Sport

PURPLE JESUS

Made for Success Publishing
P.O. Box 1775 Issaquah, WA 98027
www.MadeForSuccess.com

Distributed by Blackstone Publishing

First Printing
Library of Congress Cataloging-in-Publication data
    Author Jesus, Purple
    A Pickleball Gospel: The Harmony of Competition and Cooperation in Sport
       p. cm.

LCCN: 2024943814
ISBN: 978-1-64146-879-4 *(PBBK)*
ISBN: 978-1-64146-881-7 *(eBook)*
ISBN: *978-1-64146-880-0 (AUDIO)*

Printed in the United States of America

For further information, contact Made for Success Publishing
+1425-526-6480 or email service@madeforsuccess.net

"*A Pickleball Gospel* is ethnography at its finest. The book, remarkably, is both playful and scholarly and is as inviting as the sport that it masterfully describes. Manthou writes with a warm, self-aware, and genuine voice, keeping the narrative moving while thoroughly capturing the experience of competing at all levels in this burgeoning sport. Like the sport itself, *A Pickleball Gospel* is simply fun and will be enjoyed by anyone who appreciates how sport can transform lives. Sport, Manthou contends, is not just about winning, but *A Pickleball Gospel* is surely a triumph."

Richard Sosis, James Barnett Professor of Humanistic Anthropology, University of Connecticut

"Max gets it and walks it! The world of sport can hugely benefit from taking a step back to integrate this concept of "coopetition." Great moments and champions are the result."

Chris Russell, Head Men's Tennis Coach, University of New Mexico

"Pickleball uniquely explained as it relates to community and competition while maintaining playfulness and fun. A captivating read for players at all levels, as told by current pickleball professional and extraordinary human known affectionally as Purple Jesus."

Erik Lange, Professional Pickleball Player

"I've known Max since junior tennis. We are both Pacific Northwest kids. He was such a stud in high school. Two-sport athlete and a super talented kid. I've been a fan since day one, even though he used to kick my ass. Max is one of the kindest and most humble humans I know. Happy to see him making his way in pickle and doing great things."

Tyson McGuffin, Professional Pickleball Player

"Max Manthou has put together a wonderful journey for any sports enthusiast to follow his pathway into professional pickleball. His personal tone, his moments of success, and the challenges he has faced kept me engaged with his story and allowed me to feel his experiences."

Ken Herrmann, Founder and Head of International & Player Development, Association of Pickleball Professionals

This one is for Alex.

CONTENTS

THE DROP

INTRODUCTION

BEFORE ANYTHING ELSE IS SAID, I must first express my gratitude to you, dear reader, for taking time out of your life to read something that pertains to mine.

The content of this book is *ethnographic* in that it attempts to bring the community of pickleball to life with an insider's description of lived experience, but in combination with this, what follows also feels very much like my own personal love story. It is the story of my immediate family, who have poured their love into me and made everything possible. It is the story of my friends, who have loved and laughed with me as we suck the marrow of life. Finally, it is the story of sport, which has provided me with meaningful pursuit and positive social interaction, thereby saturating my life with love. By virtue of your interest, I am happy to say that this love story now includes you. With the multitude of other activities available to occupy your time, including *playing* pickleball instead of reading about it, it is my humble and sincere wish that you find something in the following pages that is worth your while.

The origins of this book and the events that sent me on a crash course with pickleball, I suppose, go as far back in my life as I endeavor to look. At a family reunion on Christmas Eve, my five-year-old self fell into my uncle's outdoor pool alone and nearly drowned. It may, in fact, be my earliest memory: the slight misstep, the shock of the cold water, the desperate flailing, and finally, the tight wrap of blankets as my mother held me in her arms in front of the fireplace, presumably after a heroic rescue that I don't remember.

The next summer, my wise parents placed me in a swimming class at a facility that also happened to have tennis. Their act of love had profound and amusing consequences. To this day, I can barely float, and I attempt to "swim" only if I'm staring down death. Yet, it is very difficult to imagine my life without racquet sports, especially tennis. Tennis would eventually bless me with a college scholarship, take me to nearly all fifty states, and shape my life through trial and friendship in a way that I could not have imagined.

Of course, just as it takes a community to raise a child, it takes an entire army of opposing competitors to raise a sportsperson. Significantly, the motivation for this book was born from one particular opposition in my career, one of intense rivalry yet also of intense respect. Going forward, I will regard this opponent simply as "my rival," though he was more than that to me. Both my rival and I hailed from the Pacific Northwest; he grew up in Oregon, and I grew up in Washington. Both of us had loving public school teachers for parents and enjoyed similar middle-class upbringings. Both of us were short for high-level athletes, and at one point or another, both of us probably would have sacrificed a kidney for a couple of extra inches so that we could quit tennis for basketball, especially if it meant we could dunk. In my rival, I had essentially found my mirror image, though an alternate, bizarro-world version who had a two-handed forehand and rooted for Ducks over Dawgs.

Our rivalry continued in college when my rival attended the University of Oregon and I attended the University of Washington, two schools that are themselves rivals. Fatefully, after playing each other over fifteen times in ten years, our careers culminated in a climactic final match in our junior year in 2013. That year, the annual conference match between the University of Oregon and the University of Washington was decided by the two of us.

To set the stage, it is important to understand how NCAA Division I tennis matches operate. Unlike most tennis formats, college tennis is largely team-based. Each match between teams starts with three doubles matches, which collectively are worth one point, awarded to the winner of the majority. Following the doubles matches, there are six singles matches, each worth one point. Team matches are thus decided from best-of-seven points. The most exciting moments occur when five of the six singles matches have finished and the team score sits at 3-3, meaning the winner of the last remaining match decides the winner of the team match overall. Because it is a collegiate setting, the rowdiness of the crowd in these situations often reaches a level that is rare for tennis and tends to add to the pressure as well.

Such was the case in 2013 when my rival and I tangoed yet again. Despite the fact that the match was played in Eugene, Oregon, in front of a very pro-Oregon crowd and that my rival had bested me in our two most recent engagements, Lady Fortuna smiled favorably in my direction. I played an inspired third set to take the match for my team, though I barely remember anything specific about the points. It was actually the moment after that I will never forget. My teammates rushed me with an enthusiasm that bordered on ecstasy. As we celebrated, however, I could not help but notice my rival utterly dejected on the bench, hunched over with a towel over his head. That image struck me as perverse in some fundamental way and provoked an uneasy feeling in the pit of my stomach, though I could not quite make sense of it at the time. I very much regret not approaching him to congratulate him on what we had accomplished through the years of friendly opposition and to thank him for being the co-star in my career. This regret was multiplied tenfold when, a few weeks later, my rival went cliff diving with a large group of University of Oregon athletes and, tragically, never came up.

The memory of our climactic encounter inspired this book in a number of ways. Looking back, it is no surprise that I felt conflicted in my team's moment of triumph, as research shows testosterone levels don't respond with the usual post-victory spikes against someone cared for; in fact, the winner's testosterone level often *drops*.[1] Yet, this was more than a neurobiological issue. I believe what my body expressed in the form of an uneasy feeling in my stomach was a recognition of the perversity of how winning and losing are commonly perceived and responded to, not just by the competitors but also by the audience and, by extension, the entire sporting world. Winning is generally rewarded with medals and prizes, while losing is generally "rewarded" with scorn. Is it fair, perhaps even natural, to do this? Could things possibly be done differently?

On a basic level, in most cases, there can be no winner without a loser, as the presence of one is necessitated by the other. In addition, the greater the strength of the loser, the better, since winning increases in value as the effort it takes to accomplish the victory also increases. Losing, therefore, plays a vital and valuable role in any competitive process. This is not to say that winning and losing should be valued equally; on the contrary, this may not even be possible. One study suggests that in approximately 75% of cases, regardless of culture, winners feel joy and satisfaction, and in an even greater number of cases, losers feel sadness and disappointment.[II] Instead, what seems to be lacking is an *appreciation* for losing that is proportionate to its value since losing is part and parcel of the competitive relationship that includes winning.

Taking the climactic match versus my rival as an example, the result may have determined that I "won," and yet our entire history of mutually constitutive acts, the push and pull of our decade-long dance, one might say, was completely hidden from the common observer. While I make no claims that we *caused* each other's respective success, our very presence as representatives of major college teams was greatly impacted by the effect of each other's continuous presence from years past. We became motivating factors by providing each other with someone to push back against, both in person and in the mind, during training.[1]

We succeeded partly, and I would argue, crucially, because the other did as well. Though we strove to outdo each other, our development was strongest when the other brought their best game. This resulted in our defeat from time to time but

---

1. Rivalry is particularly beneficial in the Pacific Northwest, where poor weather conditions create a scarcity of potential opponents.

paradoxically left us better equipped to win in the future. It is such that victory or defeat in any particular match was mostly an unimportant, arbitrary result; as long as the dance continued, success was built into our relationship *even before stepping onto the court.*

So how must we deal with "winners" and "losers" produced so definitively and peculiarly by sport? First and foremost, it is best to remember that sports results often do not reflect a true and obvious gap between competitors. Randomness always plays at least some role in the outcome of a match and is rarely properly accounted for when appraising winners and losers.[2] It is always the case that things could have been different if luck had swung a different way. Furthermore, in any tightly contested tennis match, the winner will win only slightly more than 50% of the points, which means the winner also experiences a lot of losing. The slightest change in court positioning, contact with the ball, decision-making, wind resistance, glare, or a million other considerations, if occurring at critical moments, could change the outcome of a match. Therefore, at this basic level, a result is never totally within one's control, and a win or loss may not be entirely deserved. It is possible, for example, that a couple of different bounces could have given my rival the victory instead.

It is also worthwhile to consider what goes on in sporting competitions on the micro-level. Many sporting competitions are the buildup of players exercising their fine motor skills against one another to perform at their most accurate. In

---

2. This has actually been proven in European football (i.e., soccer) with substantial overreaction to random luck in the evaluation of post-game player ratings based on post-goals and post-misses.[III]

racquet sports, this involves chasing after the opponent's offering and attempting a re-offering. The point builds with each successful re-offering and then dies when an offering is either too weak or too strong. As such, the match between my rival and I was a co-creation that built steadily over time from each mini co-creation. The irony is that, had either of us performed worse, our match would have ended earlier and with a more lopsided score, making the match both less consequential and less memorable. Instead, the match was made special due to the relatively equal output it inspired and the dramatic situation that resulted from the equal output. Thus, I did not simply "win"; I won largely because the two of us won as a pair. In fact, we were likely the most successful pair of the day.

All this is to say that winning and losing are two sides of the same coin and should be recognized as such. Success is often separate from the final outcome and lies more often in the process, from the day-to-day of one's training to the mutual construction of the moment. Barring a complete devolution into antagonism, fighting, or deliberately uninspired play (sometimes called "tanking"), each side in a competitive environment benefits mutually, though perhaps not equally, so that in the end, there is no true winner or loser. Therefore, it makes little sense to pop champagne for winners and pickle juice for losers, as entertaining as each of those acts may be.

Life moved on eventually, and I pushed through my grief to finish my senior season. After graduation, I traveled a lot, became a vegetarian, served in the Peace Corps in Indonesia, did some social work with boys from Central America, then finally decided to go to graduate school. For the research project that eventually led to this book, I returned to memories of my rival and our last dance and decided to make a tribute to it. That tribute is now at your disposal to make of it what you like, though I am aware that you may be wondering when in the world I will get to pickleball. I promise you, dear reader, that just like winter, it is coming.

1

WHAT IS PICKLEBALL?

THOUGH PICKLEBALL HAS made quite a splash in recent years, I still regularly run into people who have never played or seem to know nothing about it. The world is a big place with a lot of niches, so this makes sense. Nevertheless, I am often struck with a playfully exaggerated reaction like that of Marlon Brando in *Apocalypse Now*: "... The horror . . . The horror . . ."

On that note, first things first. The basics.

Pickleball was invented in 1965 at the house of future U.S. Representative Joel Pritchard in Bainbridge Island, Washington.[1]

---

1. This is only a short drive and ferry ride away from where I grew up. The original court is actually still intact and is often referred to as the pickleball "Mecca." Some places even decide which side of the court serves first by identifying the side that faces Bainbridge Island, an idea that plays off the *qibla* in

As the story goes, Pritchard and his friends, Bill Bell and Barney McCallum, were hoping to get their families to be more active over the summer. The three men lowered a badminton net to the ground, perforated a plastic ball, wielded ping-pong-sized paddles, and came up with rules that were a cross between tennis and badminton. Their innovation was a huge success. By the 1980s, pickleball had become a staple of gym classes across the United States, especially in the Pacific Northwest.

A pentagram of paddles and pickleballs (Image courtesy of the author.)

The game has changed only slightly since the early days. The pickleball court is still the same size as a badminton court. The balls are like bouncier wiffle balls: slightly larger than tennis balls, made of plastic, and may have approximately twenty-six or forty holes depending on whether they're made for indoors or outdoors. Paddles are about half the size of tennis racquets, have flat surfaces, and come in many different materials, namely wood, graphite, carbon fiber, and fiberglass.

During play, the ball may bounce once but not twice, like tennis. Most games go until one team scores eleven or fifteen points, win by two. In most cases, scoring may occur only on one's serve, similar to the scoring system once used in volleyball. To serve,

---

Islam. I was privileged enough to visit and play a game on the original court with friends in 2021.

players make an under-hand motion and contact the ball below their waist. Both players on a team serve until they lose their respective points, at which point the other team serves.

One of the most impor-tant and unique aspects of pickleball is the area encom-

Pickleball courts and a view of the kitchen line (Image courtesy of the author.)

passing the seven feet on either side of the net, called the "kitchen." Players cannot enter the kitchen or step on the "kitchen line" to hit a volley (i.e., strike the ball before it bounces). This means that if the ball is kept successfully in the kitchen with a series of lightly struck shots, otherwise known as "dinks," it is very difficult for opposing players to play powerfully or offensively. The kitchen effectively acts as a buffer zone where the net is too high and the court is too small for power shots to drop down and land in play. In this way, a well-placed soft or medium shot is often more likely to be effective than a ball that is crushed.

A second important rule is that the serving team cannot volley the first shot after the serve. This neutralizes the effect of the serve and allows the returning team to approach the net first. Taken together, the serving volley rule and the kitchen line make it hard for players to take an overwhelming advantage due to youth or athleticism. This noticeably shrinks the gap in performance between men and women and between players of different ages, likely contributing to the sport's popularity.

In recent years, pickleball has rapidly increased in popu-larity, with its total pool of players in the United States rising

223.5% from 2020 to 2023 to almost fourteen million.[2][iv] In a twist of fate, pickleball benefited greatly from the COVID-19 pandemic since the sport can be played in a space as small as one's backyard and is relatively affordable.[3] Many tennis courts and other sport courts have since been replaced by pickleball courts or have been generally overrun by pickleball players setting up temporary nets and temporary lines. Pickleball clubs, too, began to sprout up nearly everywhere in 2023. The overall spread has been most extensive in North America, though the sport has started to gain a foothold in Europe, East Asia, South America, and Oceania as well.

Indications of pickleball's increased public presence are numerous and seem to increase by the day. Notable events include the release of *InPickleball* lifestyle magazine in September 2021,[4] the celebrity pickleball tournament and two-hour CBS special *Pickled* hosted by Stephen Colbert in November 2022, *Pickleball Slam* events hosted on ESPN featuring a number of tennis champions in 2023 and 2024, and the proliferation of the restaurant chain Chicken N Pickle.

---

2. Much gaudier numbers between 30-50 million players (around 18% of American adults) are often cited from press releases by the APP Tour.[v] These represent an approximation of Americans who participated in pickleball at all in the twelve-month period preceding whichever press release is being cited. I prefer the more conservative estimate for "players."

3. The affordability of pickleball comes with a caveat, as companies have capitalized on the recent surge in popularity to charge what I perceive to be exorbitant prices for paddles. Any quality paddle will now cost over $100, with prices routinely reaching above $200. This is in line with the best tennis racquets, which are generally much sturdier and effective for longer periods of time. I have personally broken or significantly fractured the constitution of more than fifteen pickleball paddles in four years versus only two to three tennis racquets in my whole life.

4. *InPickleball* joins the original *Pickleball Magazine*, which has been published since 2016.

Occurring alongside pickleball's popularity surge has been the continued institutionalization of the sport, featuring the development of two competing professional tours: the Association of Pickleball Professionals (APP) and the Professional Pickleball Association (PPA). This is in addition to organized pickleball leagues, including Major League Pickleball (MLP), a professional league that expanded to Australia at the end of 2023, and Minor League Pickleball (MiLP), a constituent league for amateurs. Tens of thousands of dollars are now routinely offered at professional tournaments,[5] and this, combined with sponsorship deals, has allowed a handful of players to earn their entire livelihood by playing pickleball. There is even talk of making pickleball an Olympic sport in 2028 or 2032. As of this writing, the International Pickleball Federation has seventy-seven members, two more than the seventy-five-country requirement for a proposal to be made.[VI]

All of this indicates that pickleball has come a long way from Joel Pritchard's front yard. There are also no signs of it slowing down. At the moment, the sport is in an exciting liminal phase of rapid development in which norms, values, and expectations are being transformed for a great many players. What was once an obscure, casual diversion now offers true life-changing potential. This has been especially true in my case as well.

Pickleball came into my life at a crucial time, late in 2018, when I had returned from Indonesia and did not quite know what to do next. I had been forever changed by my experience abroad and suffered from reverse culture shock and a confusing

---

5. The PPA and MLP have featured large prize pools and lucrative contracts. Thus the sport's best players have tended to gravitate toward those organizations.

feeling of "homesickness." I desperately needed to reconnect with fellow Americans at home again. I also had hardly played tennis for three years and wasn't aware of how much I needed a new athletic endeavor. Enter pickleball and its many blessings. In providing an arena for athletic achievement, social connection, and even financial stability, I can confidently say that pickleball changed the course of my life for the better.

However, I must once more ask for patience, dear reader, as I digress away from pickleball for another moment. This book is not necessarily about pickleball but instead uses pickleball as a vehicle for an argument about sport as a whole. Inspired by Randy Pausch's *The Last Lecture*, this is my best attempt at what he would call "head fake" learning. While distracting you with a bouncy plastic ball and tales of my wandering past, I actually have something to say.

The main argument of this book is that sport is a *non-zero-sum* game. The term zero-sum game comes from game theory and refers to a situation in which one side's gain is the other side's loss so that the net benefit is zero. Because each side in sport must win or lose (or sometimes tie), it is often argued or insinuated that, mutually, there is no gain and that sport is, therefore, zero-sum. One scholar who has made significant contributions to the scholarship of non-zero-sum games, Robert Axelrod, does exactly this in his influential book *The Evolution of Cooperation*. Axelrod uses sport as a zero-sum contrast to set up his argument on non-zero-sum games:

> *"People are used to thinking about zero-sum interactions. In these settings, whatever one person wins, another loses. A good example is a chess tournament. In order to do well, the contestant must do*

better than the other player in the game most of the time. A win for White is necessarily a loss for Black. "[VII]

Regrettably, even scholars who focus solely on sport routinely fall into the zero-sum trap.[VIII] It's as if the very specific win-loss outcomes of sport hypnotically command an attention that is difficult to resist. To my mind, however, this zero-sum line of thinking about sport is superficial in the vast majority of cases, and I argue that sport is non-zero-sum in two main ways.

First and most importantly, sport is *coopetive*, meaning that it is simultaneously competitive and cooperative.[6] Sport is cooperative in obvious ways, such as coaching and teamwork, but also in non-obvious ways, such as effort, spectacle, and performing one's best. Each of these latter things requires some equal or at least opposite force to produce and are enjoyed collectively. Effort, for instance, is part of a feedback loop with an opposing effort, where an increase or decrease in intensity on one side usually has the same effect on the other. The competitive and cooperative dynamics are thus intertwined in a coopetive relationship, which greatly contributes to the non-zero-sum nature of sport.

Coopetition

Because coopetition is so heavily featured in this book, what follows is a brief history and description of the concept. An intuitive understanding of the concept is probably all

---

6. For the longest time, I failed to articulate the combined competitive and cooperative aspect of sport in a way that really made sense. It was not until an interview with Wakka that I had a breakthrough when he said, "Yeah, I get it. It's like they're *coopetive*. Totally makes sense." This is a wonderful example of knowledge creation born directly out of the ethnographic process, and Wakka deserves credit for a chunk of the main argument of this book.

that is necessary to enjoy the remaining pages, though, so if a deeper dive is not your cup of tea, by all means, skip or skim.

Coopetition, as a word, is a combination of the words competition and cooperation, suggesting their fusion. If it sounds made up, that is because it has been used almost exclusively in business and does not yet have wide-spread, interdisciplinary usage. For all intents and purposes, the concept formally began with Brandenburger and Nalebuff's book *Co-opetition* in 1996, though its roots go as far back as John Nash's writings on game theory. Since then, coopetition has generally been understood in business as simultaneous cooperation and competition as a strategy for development and competitive advantage.[IX] An example is direct competitors cooperating with each other in relation to a third-party supplier to create a win-win scenario.

Notably, the number of studies on coopetition in business seems to have exploded since 2015.[X] Coopetition is now commonly viewed as a process that arises from the mutual interaction of two or more entities. There are also competing approaches to coopetition, either as a single continuum ranging from strong competition to strong cooperation or as two separate continua that co-exist (see Figure 1) so that high competition and high cooperation may occur together.

Borrowing from the business realm, this book uses coopetition to mean the simultaneous and mutual competition and cooperation that occurs in all sporting interactions. A wide range of coopetive outcomes of sporting interactions are shown in Figure 1. The most desired (i.e., most *coopetive*) outcomes are high in both competition and cooperation and occupy the top right.

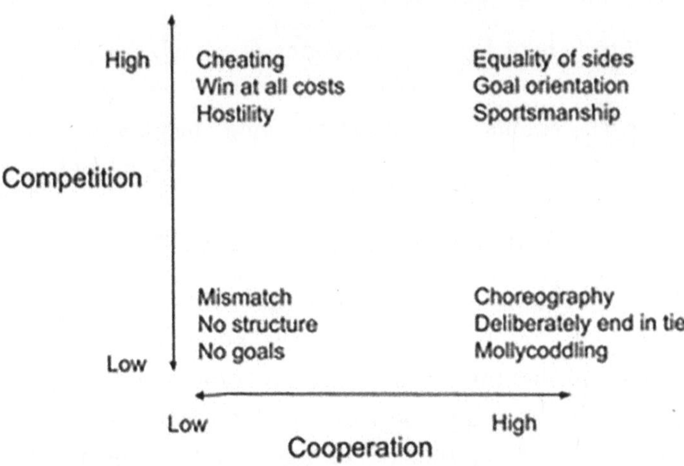

Figure 1: Coopetition as a function of competition and cooperation on separate axes. Labels indicate the extremes of each axis.[XI]

Though this is, to my knowledge, the first formal application of coopetition to sport, the concept *has* been observed in sport, most explicitly in racing by bike riders and drivers who "cooperate" through aerodynamic drafting. NASCAR champion Darrell Waltrip, in particular, is a proponent of coopetition:

> "I've used that word a million times, but nobody seems to get it. You work with the competition for the betterment of everybody. NASCAR is built on coopetition."[XII]

Many other athletes have expressed coopetive arguments without thinking of them in such terms. The basketball legend Kobe Bryant does this in *The Last Dance*, for example, when pressed on a hypothetical one-on-one matchup with Michael Jordan:

> *"I truly hate having discussions about who would win one-on-one. There are fans saying, 'Hey Kobe, you'd beat Michael one-on-one.' And I feel like, 'Yo, what you get from me is from him.' I don't get five championships without him 'cause he guided me so much and gave me so much great advice."*[xiii]

In this quote, Bryant acknowledges that the product of his labor is inseparably intertwined with that of an important mentor, which hits on a core component of coopetition. Focusing only on the competitive element of the relationship thus appears distasteful to Bryant. A second example comes from Cy Young-winning pitcher Mike Marshall, who later earned his PhD in kinesiology:

> *"Our whole society is deluged with the concept that winning is all that's important. That is bull. All that's important is that the individual does the best [they] can. Victory does not elate me, nor does defeat depress me. The only victory for me is the quality of competition, not the final score."*[xiv]

In this quote, Marshall values the quality of the collective performance over winning. In other words, "The point is to play a beautiful game," as the character Bredon says in one of my favorite fantasy book series.[xv] This is also a coopetive attitude. Put together, it is clear that the ideas behind coopetition are not foreign to sport and provide a basis for a more formal theory.

In the interest of clarity, the following example is one of the strongest accounts of coopetition in sport that I have encountered. In 2006, tennis player Andre Agassi made his last professional appearance at the US Open, making it to the third round. In the second round, a physically deteriorating Agassi defeated up-and-coming eighth-seeded Marcos Baghdatis of Cyprus in a five-set marathon that lasted over four hours. Agassi describes this match in exciting detail in his autobiography, including a post-match scenario that had him and his opponent lying on twin stretchers, both in physical agony:

"I try to watch [the TV above]. I hear moans to my left. I turn my head slowly and see Baghdatis on the next table. His team is working on him. They stretch his quad, his hamstring cramps. They stretch his hamstring, his quad cramps. He tries to lie flat, his groin cramps. He curls into a ball and begs them to leave him be. Everyone clears out of the locker room. It's just the two of us. I turn back to the TV.

"Moments later something makes me turn back to Baghdatis. He's smiling at me. Happy or nervous? Maybe both. I smile back.

"I hear my name coming from the TV. I turn my head. Highlights from the match. The first two sets, so misleadingly easy. The third, Baghdatis starting to believe. The fourth, a knife fight. The fifth, the never-ending ninth game. Some of the best tennis I've ever played. Some of the best I've ever seen. The commentator calls it a classic.

"In my peripheral vision I detect slight movement. I turn to see Baghdatis extending his hand. His face says, 'We did that.' I reach out, take his hand, and we remain this way, holding hands, as the TV flickers with scenes of our savage battle."[XVI]

In this account, there is clearly a winning pair rather than a winner and a loser. Agassi and Baghdatis pushed each other to the brink, produced a rousing spectacle, and then savored the moment together like lovers. That is coopetition at its finest.[7] While the specifics of this match are abnormally epic and not often repeated, coopetition is present in varying degrees in any sporting competition and certainly always has a similar potential.

The second way sport is non-zero-sum is through players' subjective appraisals of their own success. Winning and losing in the objective sense can have little meaning if, say, the winner comes away feeling negative about their performance and the loser comes away feeling positive. In the best of cases, such as the Baghdatis-Agassi match, both players come away feeling positive about their performance, which largely negates the zero-sum model. There is simply no straight line from winning to success or from losing to failure. It is also rarely obvious who is truly winning in the long run, even after reflecting on one's performance, as subjective evaluations of an experience can later change.

Pickleball, it turns out, has proven to be very satisfactory for the purpose of illustrating my stated argument. In fact, as a side contention, my experiences point to the possibility that pickleball is exceptionally coopetive when compared with other sports. Of course, the reader is encouraged to make their own

---

7. Again in the interest of clarity, it is important to note that coopetition differs from mere sportsmanship. Sportsmanship is generally conscious behavior toward an opponent based on idealistic beliefs of comportment in sporting contexts, whereas coopetition is more of a built-in feature of sport itself. It is true, however, that coopetition usually finds greater expression when sportsmanship is high.

judgments on the arguments I have presented here after reading the following chapters.

Borrowing from one of my favorite book series as a kid, *Choose Your Own Adventure*, you, dear reader, now have a choice:

If you want to read about the world of pickleball, turn to page 47.

If you want to read a wild tale about a pro tournament, turn to page 125.

If you want to read the damn book like it was written, turn to the next page.

2

WINNING AND WESTERN CULTURE

BEFORE DIVING DEEPER into the specifics of pickleball, I feel it is best, at this point, to address why a perspective of non-zero-sum or coopetition in sport might matter. What exactly is the benefit of these ideas? In other words, aside from some interesting documentation of pickleball, what good is it that this book exists?

As the importance of sport continues to rise throughout the world, my first thought is that healthy, or perhaps *accurate*, ideas about what is happening in sporting contexts are most desirable. Non-zero-sum and coopetition are simply ideas proposed to describe such contexts, and whether they are accurate or not is for the reader and the greater scientific community to decide. There is, however, more at play than this basic desire for accuracy.

Pickleball has its origins in Western, specifically American culture, and it is currently in those same places where enthusiasm for the sport is highest. This matters because the United States inherited and expanded upon the Western drive to compete that notoriously pushed its small yet mighty European nations to conquer the rest of the world during colonialism. In the 1960s, anthropologist Jules Henry identified the United States as a "driven culture" intent on achievement, specifically in comparison with others to get ahead,[XVII] and this competitive drive is still very much alive in the United States today. The belief in American exceptionalism is a related "affliction," one might say, as is the American obsession with winning and being number one.[1] Former US President Donald Trump frequently tried to exploit this obsession on the campaign trail in 2016, demonstrated in this statement to an adoring crowd at a rally in Billings, Montana:

> *"We're going to win. We're going to win so much. We're going to win at trade, we're going to win at the border. We're going to win so much, you're going to be so sick and tired of winning. You're going to come to me and go, 'Please, please, we can't win anymore.'... You'll say, 'Please, Mr. President, we beg you, sir, we don't want to win anymore. It's too much. It's not fair to*

---

1. This obsession with being number one was parodied in the comedy *Talladega Nights*, in which race car driver Ricky Bobby lives most of his life believing the words, "If you ain't first, you're last," spoken in his youth by his intoxicated father. He then finds out later that his (sober) father thinks those same words, are stupid: "Aw hell, Ricky, I was high when I said that! That doesn't make any sense at all! You could be second, you could be third, fourth . . . hell, you could even be fifth!"

everybody else.' And I'm going to say 'I'm sorry, but we're going to keep winning, winning, winning.' We're going to make America great again.'[XVIII]

Unsurprisingly, the obsession with winning and being better than others has made its mark in the sporting world as well. In the early years of American professional sports, it was not uncommon for high-profile athletes and coaches to embrace a "win-at-all-costs" mentality, often overtly belittling losers in the process. This fanatic position is best represented by ex-Washington Redskins coach George Allen:

"The winner is the only individual who is truly alive. I've said this to our ball club: 'Every time you win, you're reborn; when you lose, you die a little.'"[XIX]

Recently, with an increasing focus on mental health in athletics, attitudes have tempered somewhat, especially the vitriol toward losers, though the drive to win is as strong as ever. In *The Last Dance*, for example, beloved basketball legend Michael Jordan was asked if it was "gratifying" to leave the Chicago Bulls at the peak of his career following six championships in essentially six tries, to which he responded:

"It's maddening because I felt like we could've won seven. I really believe that. We may not have, but man, just not to be able to try, that's something that I just can't accept.'[XX]

A major issue with this perspective is that it contains no built-in satisfaction with winning ever being enough. However, I make mention of this not to dunk on Jordan but rather to highlight Jordan as what Jules Henry would call a "cultural maximizer" within the context of the American obsession with winning.[XXI] He is an American icon for many reasons, but a key reason is that he won.

Granted, the previous quotes are from exceptionally competitive individuals who may not represent the average American or Western sportsperson. There is nevertheless good reason to believe that these attitudes are widespread, to the point of engulfing even youth sports. Consider the reflections of ex-professional hockey player Cassidy Preston after losing a pair of games mid-season as the coach of a Canadian ten-year-old select hockey team:

"I have never been hit so hard with the pressure to win from the parents—not the players! It is just madness—as if I don't want to win—that is their mindset. They question how competitive I am. It blows my mind, really. They are not explicitly saying that 'we have to win or we will leave,' but that is the message that is being delivered."[XXII]

The obsession with winning for these parents seems out-of-place in such a young age division—or any age division for that matter—and may also extend to their children. Preston mentions that many of his players could not deal with defeat even in one-on-one drills in practice, "Apparently thinking winning was all that mattered."[XXIII]

Of course, it is possible that these anecdotes have been cherry-picked and, therefore, do not reflect a greater truth about American and/or Western culture. If nothing else, though, the fetish with winning, wherever and whenever it exists, equates "athlete" with someone who wins, thus discouraging all but the very elite performers while also valorizing high-level athletes to a standing that is much beyond their due. This has consequences for both sexes but may have a disproportionate effect on males and the construction of masculinity. Consider this passage from J.R. Moehringer's memoir *The Tender Bar*, in which Moehringer's cousin McGraw returns home to a bar in New York after becoming a star pitcher at the University of Nebraska:

"Despite the warm reception [the men at the bar] gave him, the men weren't quite sure how to take this new McGraw. Like me, they were proud and intimidated at the same time. They went back and forth between kidding him as if he were still ten and deferring to him as if he were their king. At times I thought they might weave him a crown of cherry stems and swizzle sticks.

"Cager had marched through minefields in Củ Chi [in Vietnam], Bob the Cop had dodged bullets in Brooklyn, Fast Eddy had plummeted to Earth at 150 miles/hour [as a skydiver], but they all stepped aside for McGraw that night, because becoming a pro [sic] baseball player was the summit."[XXIV]

Additionally, consider this passage from Jedidiah Jenkins's memoir *To Shake the Sleeping Self*, in which Jenkins arrives in Costa Rica with a companion after having bicycled almost the entire way from Oregon:

"I sat [in front of the harbor in Costa Rica], looking at the ocean, and felt accomplished. We had biked across an entire country, from the Pacific coast to the Caribbean coast. I felt athletic. [Some] big burly men said I was an athlete. Almost no one had ever said that about me in my life. It felt good . . . I was embarrassed that it felt so good. It soothed an old wound. My thirteen-year-old brain had made a note, 'You are not an athlete, and athletes are what you should be.' I grew up and never threw out that note. I became funny and charming and accomplished, and I collected all kinds of notes.

> *But beneath those piles of paper, the original note remained. 'You are not an athlete, and an athlete is what you should be.'"*[XXV]

Each of the previous passages displays some of the perverse social consequences of a sport-crazed culture preoccupied with winning and the athletes who do the winning. However, it's fair to wonder how sport could lead to any other state of affairs, given the nature of sport's hierarchical, win-loss outcomes. To show that a preoccupation with winning is not "natural" or inevitable in sport, consider the following passage from Michael Wesch, an anthropologist who lived in a small village in central Papua New Guinea. Wesch joined a basketball game, "own[ed] the court" with steals and flashy dunks (on an eight-foot rim), then received startlingly stern looks from a friend. He writes:

> *"I drifted into the background of the game as I tried to figure out what was going on. The other team started scoring, tying the game at 14. '14-14!' the scorekeeper announced with jubilation, pointing to his nose. Everybody cheered and walked off the court. Where's everybody going? I thought. It's tied up. 'Next basket wins!' I suggested. [My friend] took me aside. 'Mike, we like to end in a tie,' he said, and then he smiled the way you smile at a four-year-old who is just learning the ways of the world and gently recommended that I not do any more dunking. 'People might be jealous.'"*[XXVI]

The takeaway from this passage is that winning *does not have to be emphasized.* In other words, there exists the possibility of approaching sport in a way that is less zero-sum. This does not mean that winning should be demonized or abandoned as a pursuit. In fact, there is reason to believe that there is much to gain simply in the pursuit of winning. Much of sport is a Sisyphean effort of pushing the boulder of competition as far up the hill of resistance and adversity as one can go, only to see it fall back down the hill to be pushed again another day, regardless of whether one becomes a champion or not. It may be that the eagerness to push and the earnestness with which one pushes is what truly makes one a winner. Indeed, winning can even be seen as a social construction, as the villagers in Wesch's passage seem to "win" together as a group.

Putting such idealism aside, what is clear is that American and/or Western culture takes winning, in the objective sense, very seriously, and zero-sum thinking is not only rampant but also likely carries serious consequences. A non-zero-sum framework that highlights the often-hidden or overlooked coopetive elements in sport thus has much to offer. It was in the spirit of exploring a non-zero-sum framework in sport that I threw myself more fully into pickleball, though again, it is up to the reader to decide just how well the framework applies.

3

LIFTING THE VEIL

AS STATED IN CHAPTER I, I have been playing pickleball on and off since 2018, and racquet sports more generally since the wee age of six. One might assume that this has given me some wisdom about pickleball and racquet sports, given also that these are indeed my words on the page, but allow me to have a come-to-Socrates moment: I have learned enough about pickleball, sports, and the world in general to know that I don't know much. In fact, a public service announcement like the one in *South Park*, warning you, dear reader, that this work "Should not be viewed by anyone," could very well be appropriate. Alas, you have made it this far, so it's possible that you will continue. The purpose of this brief meta-chapter is to, therefore, lift the veil of my own knowledge in addition to outlining some basic structures and components of the rest of the book.

First off, though this book pulls from many points in my life, the bulk of the information comes from when I was a graduate student at Illinois State University from 2021 to 2023. For research purposes, I greatly increased my overall participation in the pickleball community from the summer of 2022 to the spring of 2023. During this time, I traveled to numerous pickleball courts at public parks, tennis centers, fitness centers, pickleball clubs, schools, and churches, mostly in the Midwest, though also in Washington, Alabama, and Florida. This enabled me to experience pickleball in many different settings and meet hordes of pickleball players from many walks of life. To help with recall, I kept detailed notes of all my pickleball encounters in a journal.[1]

Unfortunately, as Wile E. Coyote proves, experience does not guarantee wisdom, and the reader would still be wise to doubt what I actually know. On a basic level, much of my experience has been biased by my position as a white, heterosexual, able-bodied male from a middle-class family. On top of this, because I am arguably a pro-level player, I tend to receive a rose-colored view of things in the pickleball world. There are hardly any occasions in pickleball spaces where my presence is unwanted or even unnoticed. Furthermore, most players tend to be on their "best behavior" when I'm around. This can make observations of more "normal" or commonplace pickleball behavior difficult.

---

1. I usually jotted down notes the same day as events, though later at night and not in the moment as the events occurred. This approach to note-taking risks observations being less vibrant, more biased, or even incorrect. However, I find that taking notes in the moment takes me out of the moment, so to speak, and can distract others as well. On one occasion when I did try to take notes in the moment, I actually had a player get self-conscious and playfully demand to know what I was writing.

Aware of these limitations, I found it necessary to interview thirteen avid pickleball players and use their responses to build a more informed understanding of the pickleball world. Finding players willing to interview was easy—pickleball players *love* to talk about pickleball, especially over food.[2] The main difficulty was deciding who to choose among the many available options. I decided against interviewing anyone I knew intimately and settled instead for individuals who had either appeared in my pickleball life repeatedly, in small moments, or who had made a connection with me in a more meaningful, singular moment. In this way, the interviewees seemed to choose themselves, and I often felt grateful that the serendipity of life had caused our paths to cross.

In the interest of confidentiality, all interviewees and collaborators in this book, outside of those I competed against in professional events, are identified using pseudonyms of their choosing. More accurately, these pseudonyms are *pickleball nicknames*, which are a light-hearted, playful feature of the sport, especially prior to 2023. Players who choose to adopt a nickname can have their real name replaced on tournament draws, which adds to the fun.

Because I am frequently asked about my own pickleball nickname, here is a quick explanation. In the process of registering for a tournament on the old website, pickleballtournaments.com, entering something in the blank space for "Nickname" in one's online profile would actually

---

2. Some of the most meaningful spaces in pickleball are what I call "pickleball communions" with other players post-play. These communions are often highly social events filled with enthusiastic pickleball talk that allow players to relive the highlights and process what just occurred.

replace one's real name at a tournament, though there was no indication of this.[3] Reasoning that my profile would never be seen by anyone, my ignorant 2019 self wrote the last nickname that I had in college. Imagine my shock, then, when the front desk yelled out "Purple Jesus!" at my first tournament when it was my time to play. Ever since then, I have been known in the larger pickleball community as Purple Jesus, which has been modified to "Purple" or "PJ" at various times. Originally an accident, I have since embraced it.[4]

Interviewees and other individuals who appear in the upcoming pages are listed here in the following tables:

Name	Age	Level	Note
Air Pickleball	50+	3.5-4.0	Sports junkie who became the first state qualifier from his high school in tennis. Husband to Rowdy Ria. Co-leader of a pickleball club at his church.
Bad Boy	35+	5.0	Former college tennis player with a nifty left hand.

3. The new tournament registration website, pickleballbrackets.com, does not have the nickname space on one's profile, which has singularly contributed to the disappearance of nicknames more than anything else. There is still no issue with writing a nickname in the "Name" space, however.
4. I thoroughly enjoy nicknames and stage names. My junior tennis coach (and quasi-older brother) gave me the nickname "Little Big Man" from age ten to eighteen, which I had written on numerous shirts and hats. In college, tennis teammates of mine liked to play with my last name, Manthou, and called me "Manthong," which was shortened to "Thong" or "Tong" on occasion. "Purple Jesus" eventually emerged as a combination of my penchant for wearing purple, my long hair and big nose, and my love for the character of the same name in *The Big Lebowski.*

Name	Age	Level	Note
Beautiful	60+	5.0	One of the original pickleball players, with over thirty years of experience.
Big Cat	19+	5.0	Former college basketball player and an old soul.
Bullet	50+	3.5-4.0	Non-sportsman for most of his life besides semi-professional paintball in his younger years. Plays pickleball 5x/week. Mixed doubles partner to KO.
Condor	35+	4.5-5.0	Multi-sport athlete with long arms who gets paid to save lives.
Flash	35+	Pro	Former recreational tennis player with lightning-fast hands.
Juke	35+	5.0	Former soccer player with a fiery intensity on the court.
KO	50+	3.5-4.0	Music enthusiast and former recreational tennis player. Started pickleball right after COVID. Plays 5x/week. Mixed doubles partner to Bullet.
M1	50+	4.5-5.0/ Senior Pro	Current mid-to-high level tennis player who tried everything in high school. Found pickleball about one year ago and now plays nearly every day. Hits excellent slices.
Maverick	50+	4.0-4.5	Avid athlete in early life who found golf and frisbee golf after high school. Plays pickleball 5x/week and drills with a ball machine. Improved from 2.5 level. Travels often for tournaments.

Name	Age	Level	Note
The Mayor	35+	4.5-5.0	Former D1 NCAA football player. Also a track athlete and Little League slugger. Really got into pickleball during COVID. Often drills by himself on a wall in his basement to improve.
Nasty	19+	Pro	Pickleball coach with a wicked backhand volley flick.
Ninja	19+	5.0	Former college tennis player and childhood friend of mine.
Nuke	60+	4.0-4.5	Highly active sportsman post-high school. Once bowled a 300 in officially sanctioned league play. Plays pickleball 3x/week and nurses knee pain. Prefers singles.
Papa Rosey	60+	4.0	Former college wrestler and father of Rosey.
Pickle Bella	50+	3.0-3.5	Recreational athlete with the best memories in volleyball. Improved from absolute beginner by taking lessons for a year. Now plays 5x/week. Highly social.
Ping Pong Mike	35+	5.0	Former 1700-level table tennis player who has tried nearly every sport. Very competitive in sports but much less so in life. Played for over fifteen years.
The Professor	35+	4.5-5.0	Former tennis player with a trademark phrase (good shootin').

Name	Age	Level	Note
Py	60+	4.5-5.0	Former college tennis player with a kind heart.
Rocky	60+	3.5	Handsome and charming brother to Papa Rosey.
Rosey	19+	Pro	Highly athletic pickleballer with a jovial personality.
Rowdy Ria	50+	3.0-3.5	New sportswoman, though has always been a loud supporter of others. Plays pickleball 5x/week. Wife to Air Pickleball. Co-leader of the pickleball club at her church.
Sharpy	19+	4.5-5.0	Former tennis player with a beautiful family.
Suzy Q	35+	4.5-5.0	Former college softball player and current racquetball player. Once hit a walk-off in the state tournament. Known for fighting spirit. Plays 3x/week. Hits unique backhand dink due to unusual bone structure.
Thor	19+	Pro	Recent D1 NCAA tennis player. Certified pickleball coach. Hopes to earn enough as a pro to be full-time, though not fixated on being number one.
Wakka	35+	4.5-5.0	Former taekwondo, racquetball, and mountain biking enthusiast. Plays 4x/week. Organizes informal weekly tournaments. Very proud of his family.

Note on Levels/Ratings

The ratings used in the table are based on the most basic pickleball rating system in the United States, the USA Tournament Player Rating (UTPR), which works similarly to the rating system used by the United States Tennis Association. Skill levels are listed in increments of 0.5 and can theoretically rise to be as high as 6.0. Practically speaking, anyone with a wit of athletic ability will be at least 2.0 after only a few tries. The largest glut of regular players tends to be 3.0 to 4.0, with the ranks quickly thinning out beyond that.

For tournament events, the lowest level offered is generally 3.0 and the highest level is 5.0, with anything above that just considered "Pro" (or "Senior Pro"). Events are divided by form (singles, doubles), gender (men's, women's, and mixed), and level (3.0-Pro), then often by age (19+, 35+, 50+, 60+, etc.) if the number of registered teams is large enough. Once a player has played a "sanctioned" (i.e., official) tournament, they receive UTPR ratings for each type of event they played (singles, doubles, mixed doubles), which update digitally based on their results.

Alternatively, a very similar rating system to UTPR called the Dynamic Universal Pickleball Rating (DUPR) has become the rating system of choice for many players and tournaments since 2022. Unlike UTPR, DUPR rates players regardless of gender and uses a scale that goes to about 7.0 (as opposed to 6.0). This means that players, especially men's players, have a slightly higher DUPR rating than UTPR rating with things being accurate.

Going forward, the chapters of this book progress like a pickleball player's journey through the different stages of the game. Players must first enter the game (Chapter IV), then play enough to begin to identify themselves with it (Chapter V). Players may first mix in with other community members at a local park (Chapter VI), then start to attend more structured "Open Play" events (Chapter VII). From there, they may connect with a core group of others and start to play more privately (Chapter VIII). Eventually, players may develop enough skill and determination to want to compete in a local tournament (Chapter IX), then in a tournament with monetary prizes or higher stakes on the line (Chapter X). Finally, some players may be privileged enough to test their skills at a professional event (Chapters XI-XII).

The following chapters also utilize a variety of perspectives. Each chapter begins with a vignette from my personal experience, and special effort is made to describe how pickleball sounds, smells, and feels. After these vignettes, the core of each chapter is written in a narrator's voice, with a great many quotes from interviewees mixed in for support. Finally, in Chapter XI, and occasionally at other times, my personal experience is used as direct source material for analysis—an exercise in what the social sciences call *autoethnography*.

Believe it or not, using the first-person perspective has traditionally been a bogeyman in anthropology and the social sciences. The self used to be seen as too subjective to be anything other than a contaminant of true, scientific knowledge. Luckily, attitudes have shifted, and I chose to write a partial autoethnography in hopes of capturing the raw performance aspect of pickleball. It also would have been a wasted opportunity not to feature my subjectivity somewhat, considering how few others can speak on the game from its highest levels.

Finally, it is now necessary to comment broadly on anthropology and speak directly to readers who may not know much about it. Though there are nifty definitions out there, with most of them focusing on culture and human evolution, what I usually tell people is that anthropology is a close cousin of sociology and that both try to say something about human societies and the human condition. The difference is that sociology tends to look at large data sets and the like, much like looking at the beach to say something about a grain of sand—the individual. Meanwhile, anthropology generally looks at the grain of sand and tries to say something about the beach. In this case, my experience in pickleball is the grain of sand, and I am attempting to say something about pickleball as a whole (a sand castle, let's say) and about sport as a whole—the beach.

Furthermore, if we, for the moment, accept the so-called "hard" and "soft" division of science, one could argue that anthropology is the softest of the sciences. This means that there is a thin line separating it from, say, literature, or any number of the arts. I find this very appealing. I have come to acquire a deep appreciation for the border places, liminal zones, and marginal entities in the world.[5] It seems that whenever

---

5. My appreciation for the marginal first developed in an undergraduate class that infused my academic life with renewed meaning and purpose, Baltic History, taught by the wonderful head of the Baltic Studies program at the University of Washington, Guntis Šmidchens. Learning about the three small but proud Baltic countries caught between Germany and the Soviet Union caused me to see the world in a new light and also convinced me to join the Peace Corps.

there is a kind of uncertainty between where one thing ends and another thing begins, such as the boundary between the sciences and the arts, a wondrous and meaningful kind of chaos occurs. (If you don't believe me, I implore you to search for the Mandelbrot Set on YouTube). Therefore, what follows is somewhat of a marriage between art and science that I hope, at the very least, will be half as entertaining for you to read as it was for me to research.

Without further ado, I present to you, dear reader, an ethnography of pickleball.

PART II

THE SPEED UP

4

FIRST FORAY INTO THE GAME

I AM SITTING ON MY COUCH on a Sunday afternoon in 2018 with the TV tuned in to a Seattle Seahawks game, though my attention is mostly directed at my phone and the progress of my fantasy football team. The game goes to commercial, and I notice something unusual—an advertisement for Pickleball Central, a pickleball superstore in Renton, Washington. Huh. Strange. Pickleball has always been just a blip on the radar. A backyard game or middle school P.E. activity. Did the world change that much when I was in the Peace Corps? Apparently, it did, because shortly afterward, I get a call from one of my best friends and fellow tennis player, Ninja, beseeching me to come play pickleball with a group he's gotten involved with.

Sounds fun! It will probably be a one-time thing, of course, or maybe an occasional diversion, but nothing more than that.

After all, it's just pickleball.

A few days later, I drive an hour north from Tacoma to meet him at a fitness center. I already feel somewhat silly for driving so far for pickleball, and then the fitness center charges me twenty-five dollars to play because I'm not a member. Wonderful. I go to the basketball gym, where they've added lines and a portable net, and I meet up with Ninja. His play-mates are all older than forty, with one gentleman actually in his sixties, and the vibe is light-hearted and fun. They seem like capable players, though I fully expect to have the upper hand after an hour or so when I start to get a feel for the game. After all, I'm a menace with a racquet in my hand, and I'm in my prime.

Then play starts, and I lose.

Then I lose again. And again. I'm not terrible, but I get the sense that everyone is sort of playing around with me like I'm an object of amusement. Then, in a rally where all four players come up to the kitchen line, Ninja dinks rather low crosscourt to the sixty-year-old, who proceeds to casually flick a one-handed backhand volley from below the net in an upward sweeping motion, right in my direction. It defies physics. I gyrate uncomfortably and make a little yelp, though the ball gets past me well before I can react. Before, I was losing, but now, I'm losing and I feel almost helpless about it. What *was* that? And what's going on here? I guess I'll have to play some more to find out.

* * *

One's journey as a pickleball player must begin somewhere, and although many new participants express great enthusiasm for the sport after their initial play, the step to begin play in the first place is commonly done amid some resistance. This resistance was especially common before COVID-19, though it has lessened somewhat in the years since as pickleball has become more mainstream. The resistance is generally due to one of two factors:

1) The perception that pickleball is primarily for the elderly
2) The perception that pickleball is silly or casual due to its optics or its name

For the first fifty years, pickleball's player pool indeed featured mostly retirees. In recent years, the sudden influx of millions into the sport has shifted the demographics to be more representative of all ages. To be sure, the elderly still participate in large numbers, but age is now less of a defining feature of the sport and more of a testament to its wide appeal. Nonetheless, ageist prejudice still lingers.

Interestingly, it can be a defeat by an elderly or older player that motivates new pickleball players to keep playing. Maverick, for instance, was initially resistant to pickleball along ageist lines ("Isn't that for *old* people?"), but then found herself motivated to take lessons after getting her "butt kicked" against a seventy-nine-year-old woman. In my own case, I still credit my butt-kicking versus the sixty-year-old gentleman as a serious factor in capturing my interest when I first entered the game.

Resistance due to the perceived silliness or casual aspect of pickleball starts first with its unusual name. Unlike other "-ball" sports, whose names are informative and to the point, such as basketball, volleyball, or football, pickleball conjures up images of a rather slimy, phallic fruit-vegetable, which incidentally has nothing to do with the sport at all.[1] Bullet, for example, was resistant to pickleball in this manner after being invited by a friend:

> *"I said, 'What the heck is pickleball?' Like, it sounds stupid. I had no idea. He's like, 'C'mon out!' And I'm like, 'I'm not coming out for that.' "*

In some cases, the sport just doesn't appear formidable or legitimate. Consider the phrase, "It's just pickleball," which is uttered on almost a daily basis on the pickleball court or in conversations around the game, usually to diffuse tension when someone is overly worked up. In tennis, one rarely hears, "It's just tennis," but instead, "It's just a game." The difference is subtle yet significant. "It's just a game" reminds the player that, at the end of the day, all games are unworthy of negatively affecting one's mental health in any serious fashion. "It's just pickleball" is more specific and suggests that pickleball itself is unworthy. In other words, it's not just because pickleball is a game, but because it is a specific *kind* of game that one should just relax and enjoy themselves.

Resistance to pickleball from a legitimacy standpoint seems to be most common among tennis players, likely for reasons to which I can personally attest. The plastic, hole-filled ball, the prolonged dinking rallies, and the miniature size of everything were all very difficult for me to take seriously. It felt like a Fisher Price version of my beloved, more mature sport. Even now,

---

1. There is a dispute over whether the sport was named after Joel Pritchard's dog "Pickle" or after a "pickle boat" that the dog was likely named after. It's like pickleball's chicken-or-the-egg dilemma.

despite a profound appreciation for the virtues of pickleball and near-full conversion away from tennis, I must fight a bias that considers pickleball somehow lesser from time to time.[2]

New entrants who break the barrier, so to speak, and find pickleball to their liking, also tend to *really* find it to their liking. "Hooked right away" is a common refrain, and it is not hyperbole. Consider Air Pickleball and Rowdy Ria. After initially resisting their friends' pleas to play, they finally met them on the pickleball court and liked their experience so much that they purchased paddles online before they had even left the court. They then drove to every location that offered pickleball on Google Maps within an hour of their house.

Even those who are lukewarm about pickleball at first but continue to play are susceptible to catching the bug at a later date. This was the case for Pickle Bella, who was first invited by her elderly neighbors:

> *"So, we go over there, and I'm thinking 'Eh, maybe once or twice a month'. . . then next thing I know, I'm doing it every day. I'd lay in bed, and I'd be like [makes stroke motions] playing pickleball. It's like, oh my god, you're obsessed."*

I, too, experienced the addictive nature of the game, though perhaps on a milder scale than many others. Suddenly, there came a day when I realized my weeks were saturated with pickleball, yet I was still looking forward to the next playdate. It's as if there's a law of *increasing* marginal returns, with each additional input of energy producing more and more pleasure and desire to keep playing. This can be characteristic of all sports,

---

2. This is a very light form of what anthropologists call *ethnocentrism*, which is judging another culture by the standards of one's own.

of course, but its flavor and frequency in pickleball are at least notable and might be unique.

One reason players feel "hooked" by the sport is that pickleball has a very gentle learning curve. Even total beginners with physical restrictions or limited athletic experience may find it manageable to play real points after only half an hour. This is in stark contrast to a sport like tennis, which requires not only a decent fitness level but considerable time and effort to refine one's fine motor skills until one is truly able to play the full game. In a good example of this, M1 describes introducing pickleball to a friend with low fitness and without significant racquet experience:

> *"When we went out to Palm Springs, we were staying with a friend of mine. He's out of shape—he's had some back problems—and I invited him to come out and play some pickleball. He said, 'Oh no, I can't do that.' And I said to him, 'You can do it, just trust me.' So, we went out there, and we were out there for over an hour, and he was learning how to hit, and he was having a blast!"*

Of course, the learning curve is especially gentle for players coming into the game with racquet skills, as they may jump levels after mere weeks or months of playing. This is true in Thor's experience, as his rate of improvement after playing just a few times was "crazy" and a primary driver for his continued participation. In fact, Thor was so encouraged that he left college tennis early and transitioned to playing professional pickleball full-time.

Wakka, an ex-racquetball player,[3] was similarly encouraged and shares his experience with the pickleball learning curve as follows:

---

3. While racquetball is a racquet sport and does help players transition to pickleball, it can also provide a serious challenge due to the difference in strokes between

"You can play competitive [quickly]. . . It makes you feel like Michael Jordan in the beginning, especially if you bring some talent to the court. Man."

While it might take racquet skills to get the "Michael Jordan" feeling in the beginning, the gentle learning curve is not exclusive to such players. New players of all shapes and sizes can still improve at rapid rates. Air Pickleball speaks on this in reference to Rowdy Ria, who had never seriously played a sport before:

"If you'd seen her play when we started, even just since this past summer, she's gotten so good . . . I play with her sometimes and I'm like, who is this? . . . There's points where she's doing all the work and I'm just watching. I'm like, who is this? That happens a lot playing with her."

Ultimately, the takeaway is that once people push past their possible prejudices and give pickleball a chance, it has a tendency to hook them in, partly by offering easy paths to competence and improvement. New players must obviously be nurtured by coaches or more skilled players, but it takes very little time for players to reach a competitive level necessary for coopetition to really kick in and bear fruit.

---

the two sports. Players with racquetball experience may suffer from old habits and struggle to hit topspin, which is crucial to success in pickleball at the higher levels.

5

PICKLEBALLERS

I GET PICKED UP outside of my parents' condo by my friend Beautiful in a cosmic blue Subaru, who tells me to thank my sister for making her baklava. We drive thirty minutes to a sports complex to play pickleball like we often used to do before I left for graduate school. We have much to catch up on, as I have not seen her since she officially turned sixty. Beautiful is a retired CFO with a kind heart, a fondness for literature, and a penchant for gossip. She also has wobbly knees that will eventually need surgery. When we play, I cover most of the court, though she can hang with the best of them with an absolute cannon of a backhand volley.

The group we meet up with is an informal "league" of twenty-four players rotating between four available courts, and

I am greeted warmly by some old friends and acquaintances upon arrival. It's roughly an even gender split, as well as a veritable hodgepodge of ages, body types, and personalities. Livelihoods vary greatly, too. There is a firefighter, a broadcaster, a tavern owner, a pastor, and a tennis coach, though these are only the ones I know. There are many I don't know, but I would not be surprised if their occupations were equally eclectic.

One player with whom I am unfamiliar takes his position across from Beautiful and me, partnering with a fit woman in her mid-thirties. We start playing, and I am immediately impressed with his skills. He has a muscular, athletic build, and I later learn that he played rugby for Tonga. The ball zips around the court as we engage in friendly yet ferocious competition. Our partners do an admirable job of keeping up, and the points are easily the most fun of the day. When it's over, we touch paddles, simmer noiselessly in dopamine, and then mix and match with other players.

The league runs for nearly three more hours before we are replaced by a group of Polynesian pickleball players. It's not long before our sounds of joy and exertion are matched by theirs. As I leave, I notice that their group may have up to three generations represented on the court, as their most enthusiastic player is a fifteen-year-old boy.

* * *

Once a new participant plays with enough regularity, they effectively become a "pickleballer." With the popularity boom of the sport, there are a lot more pickleballers than ever before.

This phenomenal increase in the player pool raises quite a few questions. Who exactly are these pickleballers? Does it make sense to refer to pickleballers as a homogeneous group? Might there be any common characteristics that make one more likely to become a pickleballer?

First, let's start with the statistics. According to data from the Sports and Fitness Industry Association, men outnumbered women in pickleball 60.5% to 39.5% in 2021, though women's 17.6% growth bested men's 13.0% growth, indicating that this gap is narrowing.[XXVII] On the ground, the gender participation gap is only noticeable at tournaments, as women's draws are often smaller than the men's. This is especially true at the 4.5 and 5.0 levels. However, in large gatherings of casual play (also called "rec," short for recreation), it is common to see a fifty-fifty split, or women may even have a majority. Gender overall does not seem to be a significant differentiating factor, especially in comparison to other popular sports such as basketball.

As for age, the largest demographic remained 55+ at 19.8% in 2021, though this was tailed closely by 18-34 at 18.5%.[XXVIII] Furthermore, the average age went down nearly a full two years to 38.1, and the fastest-growing demographic was <24 years, suggesting pickleball is getting younger. Indeed, a 2023 report by the APP cites the average age of "avid" pickleball players to be 34.8 years, with 72% of adults playing at least once a month being younger than 44 years old.[XXIX] Clearly, pickleball is no longer dominated by the elderly, and the relatively equal rate of participation from young and old folk alike shows that age is also not a differentiating factor.

On the topic of race and socioeconomic status, 73% of players were Caucasian in 2021, with African Americans and

Asian Americans only comprising 7% and 5%, respectively.[XXX] Players tend to be wealthy as well, with 45% of players earning at least $100,000 annually and 76% earning at least $50,000 in 2021.[XXXI] Both of these facts are concerning from a diversity and equality perspective and tend to go underreported amid the fervor that pickleball currently enjoys.

Though pickleball's racial and socioeconomic skew is no trifling matter, I have little more to say on the issue other than that I see no logical reason for it to persist. Pickleball can be enjoyed by all at a low price, so long as the weather is nice, and I have never seen any type of gatekeeping in pickleball spaces freely open to the public. A greater number of players from diverse racial and socioeconomic backgrounds would certainly be a welcome addition.

What *is* quite interesting for the purposes of this book is that different genders, ages, body types, athleticisms, and fitness levels seem to compete together with relative ease and harmony. What is it that allows so many different types of bodies to enjoy pickleball together?

For part of the explanation, we turn to the concept of "motility,"[XXXII] which, for our purposes, will be defined as the "bodily potential for action."[XXXIII] An organism is *motile* if it possesses the potential to move on its own (e.g., sea sponges are *not* motile). Since motility is a potentiality, humans can refine their motility through training. When I lived in Indonesia, for example, some of my friends could eat semi-comfortably with their feet, whereas I could not even bring my foot to my mouth. This is because their years of lived experience trained them for greater flexibility in the lower extremities. This habitual repetition is the basic concept behind athletic training as well.

Pickleballers, like all athletes, bring a range of motilities to the court, but what could be considered special about pickleball is that the degree of motility required to be successful is generally within reach for a great many people. Even if one brings what would qualify as elite-level motility in most contexts, pickle-ball neutralizes this would-be advantage, at least somewhat, while at the same time, the sport also bolsters the effectiveness of lesser motilities. This is done primarily through the sport's lightweight equipment, the court's diminutive overall size, and the kitchen line, the latter of which most strongly prevents more motile players from fully profiting from their advantage. Consider the words of first-time sportswoman Rowdy Ria as she compares her early experiences in pickleball to tennis.

> *"It's just not fun chasing balls . . . And I like the fact it's a smaller court. I can handle the paddle, the ball wasn't too heavy, and the court that we played in was already fenced in, so you couldn't really .chase it too far . . . It was a sport that we could *play/manage together* [said in unison with her husband]."*

For Rowdy Ria, the sport of pickleball was both accessible and manageable and has allowed her developing motility to compete favorably with other motilities. Such would not be the case for her in a great many other sports. She would not be strong enough for football, tall enough for basketball or volley-ball, fit enough for soccer, fast enough for track, coordinated enough for softball, and the list goes on. Pickleball, though? *That* she can do, and do it well.[1]

---

1. The manageability of pickleball also contributes to a sometimes comic phenom-enon of self-delusion. Pickleballers routinely think they are better than they are,

However, most pickleballers are not first-time sportspersons like Rowdy Ria and are, in fact, "converts" from a variety of other sports. Even "OG" pickleballers who started playing well before the recent explosion are unlikely to be pickleball-only or even pickleball-mainly athletes. The most obvious source of pickleballers are the racquet sports—namely tennis, table tennis, and racquetball—but the ratio of these as a group is only really significant at the highest level. Racquet skills are helpful but not required for successful play, nor are they a guarantee of success.[2]

Instead, groups of pickleballers are most likely to be diverse assemblages of athletes from non-racquet sports. The thirteen interviewees included in this book, for instance, played a whopping twenty-four different sports prior to pickleball, with previous primary sports being as diverse as football, bowling, softball, taekwondo, and paintball. To some extent, one's last or dominant sport becomes attached to one's identity as a pickleballer, especially if the player is new or if the sport is particularly relevant (such as tennis). It is not uncommon to hear, "Oh, this is so-and-so. They're new. They're a [insert sport] player."

---

more so than any other athletes I have known. There's often a very real feeling that one can hang with better players, as the gaps in ability between players are subtle. There's also no dunk, or massive tackle, or forty-yard sprint, or 100 mph pitch, or 125 mph serve that clearly separates the best from the rest. It's easy to watch even the pros and think, "Oh, I can do that!"

2. I don't want to undersell the effect of pre-developed racquet skills on play. For example, the similarity between tennis and pickleball is strong enough to have allowed me to start as a 4.0 immediately upon my first strike of the ball. It also allows for greater ease on many shots. The point is that not starting with racquet experience is not an overwhelming impediment, not even for the higher levels.

Attracting and converting a bevy of sporty people suggests that pickleballers are likely to be, or may even need to be, competitive.[3] Indeed, competitiveness is espoused by all thirteen interviewees, with only one taking a milder tone, calling themselves a "quiet competitor." Coincidentally, this is also how I might describe myself, and I thrive in competition. Thus, for pickleballers, competitiveness may be a vital part of "just what the devil they think they're up to."[XXXIV] For The Mayor, competitiveness was the main driver for him to continue playing, especially after perceiving a "manhood challenge" when he was told he could no longer play with a group because he was not good enough. For Bullet, competitiveness also drove him to continue playing, and he suspects it is a motivator for others, too:

> *"When I started playing, I was 3.0 [and] there were like three or four guys I couldn't do anything against. It so enraged me that I was bound and determined that I was going to rise above their level. So, I got the pickleball machine. Put the time in. And yes, when I play in my little hometown, those people can't touch me now . . . And it's satisfying. But I found that [in a different place], with some of the guys, it's almost an unspoken rivalry . . . Like, I'm gonna beat that guy . . . It's nothing personal. We go out, we talk, we have fun, but when we get on the pickleball court, [we're] bound and determined to beat that person. Bound and determined."*

---

3. Often, the word "competitive" is used in common speech to suggest that someone is actually *too* competitive. In other words, a "competitive" person will do anything they can to win and may even need to win. For me, someone who is competitive simply enjoys the challenge of facing an adversary, regardless of the result. As I've grown older, I've actively tried to become less competitive in the first sense while remaining just as competitive in the second sense.

Competitiveness complements the second key ingredient for pickleballers, which is obvious within minutes of most pickleball spaces: sociability. Pickleballers are remarkably sociable. Those who are not sociable stand out, like the black sheep of the pickleball world. At one tournament I played, there was a singles player in my bracket who showed up with a hoodie worn compactly around his head, talked to no one, lost two matches, and then left. I remember this inconsequential occurrence because it was so out of the ordinary, especially for an amateur event.

The social and competitive aspects at the heart of pickleball wonderfully coalesce in a quote from Wakka:

> *"One of the things that I've always loved about pickleball—you know, I've put a fair amount of thought into this—[is that] I think you have to be competitive. Those people that you see on the court on a regular basis, that love pickleball, I would put that as one of the first ingredients: you have to be competitive. Two, the social piece of it . . . Early on, when I started investing time [at the community center] and learning about some of the seniors, I found how embracing they were. Then they got to know my son, like I could take [him] there. You walk into that environment that's like cheers, [Wakka]! [Son]! I'm like, this is awesome! And that was high quality time for me to spend with my family and/or extend that to people that I liked."*

The pickleballer, therefore, is at once competitive and sociable (i.e., cooperative), in a word, *coopetive*. Intriguingly, in anthropology, the perspective of *structuralism* highlights the tendency of the human mind to think in "binary oppositions" (e.g., hot/cold, light/dark, win/loss), and it may be that pickleball's peculiar ability to diffuse the binary opposition between competitive and cooperative lends it some of its appeal. In some sense, pickleball makes athletes out of non-athletes (e.g., Rowdy Ria: "I don't even consider myself an athlete"),[4] since the desire to compete and to be social is more important than any physical characteristic.

To conclude, "pickleballer" really has the potential to extend to almost anyone; the barrier for entry is that low. Though pickleballers are, at the moment, more likely to be Caucasian and of higher socioeconomic status, the coopetive aspect seems much more foundational and less likely to change. Anyone with some spare time, the will to win, and a smile is properly qualified.

---

4. In May of 2023, sportswriter Rick Reilly mockingly commented on pickleball's ability to make athletes out of non-athletes after giving the game a try: "[Pickleball] was a lot of people who hadn't played a sport in thirty years suddenly thinking they're *athletes*. 'Man, three hours of pickleball today,' my buddy will say. 'It was epic.'"[xxxv] The irony is that making athletes out of non-athletes is one of pickleball's greatest virtues.

6

PICK-UP GAMES

IT IS THE DAY after a grueling first taste of high-level singles competition in the APP Chicago Open and my body hurts, an ominous sign that I am not Tuck Everlasting. Nevertheless, I find myself on pristine purple courts at a public park in a Chicago suburb, preparing for the next day's doubles with Condor, Juke, and Juke's dad. The four of us are enjoying perfectly comfortable weather as the only occupants of the park, aside from an elderly couple idling on a bench. I fight through spasms of stiffness in my butt and lower back while I rotate in and out of skinny singles with Condor and Juke. The ball flies around, and the competition is fun and friendly.

Meanwhile, the elderly couple starts to circle the courts on a leisurely stroll. After one point, I stop in the corner of the court and notice the elderly man taking an interest in our activity.

Amiably, I yell out a greeting and ask him if he's played before. The interaction stalls as it becomes clear he doesn't speak English. He comes closer, and we try to mime out a conversation.

"You from Russia?"

"No," he says, "U-kraine." He crinkles his face. "Putin." Then, he makes a gun-to-the-head gesture.

I laugh anxiously, thinking of the war. "This is pi-ckle-ball," I say, motioning to the ball and the paddle. "You." I motion to him, then ask, "Play?"

He gets the message and eagerly makes his way around the gate and onto the court. He is wearing sweatpants and sandals, and judging by his number of missing teeth, he must be in his late sixties or older. I hand him a spare paddle and start tapping the ball to him. He can rally! At least somewhat, and he is thoroughly enjoying himself regardless. After about seven minutes, he gets so caught up in the fun that he runs forward for a ball and completely tumbles over. Hurriedly, we help him up, and though he is still smiling, he takes this as his cue to stop. We resume skinny singles, and he and his wife watch us for another fifteen minutes before going on their way with a wave.

* * *

Once someone becomes a pickleballer, they will likely play a lot of rec games. The meat-and-potatoes of rec play in pickleball is called *Open Play*, though first, we shall discuss a specialized form of Open Play that I like to call "pick-up" (not unlike pick-up basketball). Pick-up occurs most often at public parks where courts are free for use throughout the day. Any time pickleballers go to the park to play, they open themselves up to a possible pick-up situation. Playing in games with total strangers is not uncommon, and there is usually a general expectation that players will rotate on and off after each game if all the courts are full. Within this environment, approaching others to ask for games is rarely awkward.

For some athletes coming from other sports, the pick-up setting is counterintuitive. Tennis players, for instance, have a code that is generally more standoffish. Tennis courts are usually claimed by private pairs or groups, with the expectation that said groups will get off the court after a specified (or sometimes unspoken) amount of time if there are others waiting to play, say an hour and fifteen minutes or so. M1's first experience with pickleball reflects this difference, as he and his wife arrived on her birthday at pickleball courts overflowing with players. Discouraged, they were about to leave when a man who had just finished playing and was on his way out stayed with them and introduced them to the rotations.

In many cases where the number of players exceeds the number of available spots, a rotational system is used in which players place their paddles in a queue, either on a flat surface (usually the ground) or in some pre-made, three-dimensional apparatus. Paddles are usually piled in groups of four, making full doubles pairings easy to establish once a court is open. Other variations include separate queues for separate purposes, such as one queue for more casual play and another queue for a "king's court" format, in which only the winners stay on the court. Queue systems like these make it very easy for newcomers to integrate and for all players to mix around and experience a variety of games.

For many players, pick-up offers a way to escape isolation and make human connections. In this way, I have heard from multiple sources that pickleball literally "saves lives" or has saved the life of someone specific.[1] Ping Pong Mike, for example, calls pickleball his "cure" for an especially anxious time in his life, which he attributes mostly to social isolation. Similarly, Maverick, who strongly identifies as an introvert, describes her first time going to the park for pick-up as follows:

> *"I'm watching all these people get out [of their cars], and it's like, alright, here I go. I can't believe I did it. And [my significant other] was shocked that I did it . . . I stunk really bad, and I was getting my ass kicked. But I went! Then I found out when they go again, and I went again on Sunday, and the following weekend, I did the same thing. [My significant other's] like, I can't believe this, she is going to a court by herself."*

Maverick now describes herself as "way out there" and as someone who finally "has a life" after eight years of relative loneliness in her most recent place of residence. More broadly speaking, Maverick represents a class of older folk, such as "empty nesters" who have recently found the game and had their lives infused with new purpose and meaning.

Ultimately, this pick-up, Open Play-style atmosphere offers an opportunity to build or feel a sense of community. In fact,

---

1. Indeed, "Pickleball Saves Lives" is the motto of Vivus Pickleball, co-founded by a friend of mine.

this is exactly how many players describe the social aspect of the sport: pickleball is a *community*. Virtually everyone comments on the sociality of the game and its friendly atmosphere at some point, with "embracing" being a commonly employed word. Ping Pong Mike, who describes himself as "ADD with sports" from having invested time in at least eight different ones, describes his first impression of the pickleball community as "unreal" and "unlike anything [he'd] ever seen before."

In my experience, pickleball has introduced me to individuals I would never have known otherwise. Some individuals are crossovers from tennis, but for the most part, the pickleball community is distinctly its own thing. There's also usually a softer, more amicable nature to my relationships with tennis crossovers that is different from the relationship I had with them before. As for new acquaintances, I first thought of them as "pickleball friends" before they became just friends, which is a phenomenon reported by others as well. Oftentimes, these friendships are intergenerational and/or mixed-gender, such as my friendship with Beautiful.

Perhaps just as important as the connections one has already made, however, is the comforting feeling that the *potential* to meet new people is always just at the end of one's paddle. Pickleball is a potent social lubricant in the sense that it provides an activity that facilitates meaningful connection. Interacting through pickleball is both more effective and less awkward than striking up conversations in many other settings. In fact, it is so potent that new connections are often made below the level of one's consciousness. With enough games, even absentminded play may blossom into organic connection, and players may find that they have new friends without making much of an effort. Sometimes, the number of new connections can even be overwhelming, with "[First name] pickleball" entries piling up in one's contact list. Pickle Bella, for example, claims to have hundreds of these types of contacts.

Another aspect of this community building is the "conversation" of bodies moving and responding to each other in close proximity. On the one hand, the spacing between players (in doubles) is far enough that many authorities turned the other cheek during the COVID-19 six-feet social distancing ordinances. On the other hand, bodies are close enough that players can intimately feel the presence of their partners as they attempt to move as a unit in harmony. The bodies of opponents are even felt to a decent degree, with play often occurring between all four players at the kitchen line, only a few paddle lengths away. Balls actually strike bodies with relative frequency as well, which is considered a fair, if slightly disagreeable, part of the game.[2] All this adds up to what one scholar has called a "bodywork of sociation"[XXXVI] in which players build community through physical transfers of familiarity and togetherness in addition to the sociality that pickleball promotes. There can even be a "joyous physical high,"[XXXVII] in the words of one sociologist, from the feeling of being part of several bodies in action, which is most common when there are several courts going on at once.

Cycling back to the beginning of the chapter, pick-up is the purest expression of the community that pickleball provides.

---

2. This is different from other racquet sports. In tennis, for example, if a player strikes their opponent with a ball, it is customary to immediately and sometimes dramatically apologize. Deliberately hitting one's opponent is also very frowned upon, yet in pickleball, it can be part of a legitimate strategy if done below the neck.

One can visit a foreign place, go to the park, and immediately find a potential community. However, pick-up is derivative of Open Play and is, by nature, much less structured. Much of the pickleball action actually occurs in structured settings, which we will turn to now.

7

OPEN PLAY

AFTER TWO HOURS ON THE ROAD, I step out of my car at a large racquet club and feel grateful to finally be on my feet. My skin tickles, partly because of the crisp autumn air and partly because I am itching to play. I enter the facility and make my way to a newly completed pickleball area for Open Play. Passing behind the tennis courts, a dank, musty smell that I identify with indoor tennis greets me like an old friend. As I get closer to the pickleball area, the *pop* sound of a pickleball being struck becomes audible, then less and less faint, *pop* and I feel my *pop* anticipation build. I enter the *pop* pickleball *pop* area to brilliant *pop* *pop* lighting, nine courts *pop*, and *pop* a small horde *pop* *pop* of players *pop* already gathering. The *pop* sound only becomes louder and more frequent, *pop* yet somehow slips, steadily, to the back of my consciousness . . .

My plan is to play first with Maverick and then later with Rosey for some higher-level men's games. There's a minor miscommunication, however, and Rosey is already at Open Play, so Maverick and I play a few games versus Rosey and a cycle of solid partners. The play is disjointed, and I can't quite calculate the right level of intensity to employ. Rosey comes after me aggressively and with high energy, but Maverick struggles with the pace, and I feel caught in the middle between rips and dinks. Before we are able to calibrate an equilibrium that's best for the group, the courts flood with new arrivals and we are forced to rotate.

There are at least fifty people present, and organized pandemonium prevails for close to three hours. Laughter, agony, and encouragement fill the air, accompanying the wakes of players rushing this way and that. Mini yet elaborate social dances unfold on each court. The rhythms of these dances also make up the greater dance that unfolds as a result of all those present. There are many bodies playing pickleball, and yet, in a different way, there is also only one pickleball body.

I stay with Maverick for several more games against an array of opponents, ranging from a middle-aged couple near the lowest end of the skill spectrum, who struggle to win any points, to a high-level men's team, who proceeds to hit ninety percent of the balls to me in hopes of good practice. A young hotshot in a muscle shirt very boldly challenges me to singles, which I manage to sidestep. Near the end, I do get some games with Rosey, who accuses me of sandbagging[1] after he wins the final game of skinny singles. I fail to convince him that my drop in level could be due to the magic hand of coopetition finally seizing its equilibrium.

* * *

Open Play is a semi-structured setting in which pickleballers routinely meet at a certain place and for a certain amount of time. The hallmark of Open Play is that players are expected to rotate off the court when they have finished their game and often to rotate partners as well. Other formats are possible, too, such as sticking with a single partner or a system where the winners move up, but the basic idea is to mix around with different players. Because of this, Open Play is commonly divided by level so that skill levels are never too imbalanced. Open Play also varies tremendously by court surface and by the type of ball that is used, both of which can affect the experience of play and influence which players show up in the first place.

The most "old-school" of Open Play settings is the gym floor, usually at fitness clubs, schools, community centers, and churches. In nearly all of these cases, the nets and lines are temporary, with the latter overlaid using different kinds of colored tape. Nets are usually assembled in pieces and sometimes sit on wheels to be easier to shift around. Space around and between the makeshift courts is usually marginal, with players calling "ball!" and stopping play if a ball accidentally encroaches on the

---

1. Sandbagging is a general sports term that refers to purposefully performing below one's level.

wrong court, which happens just rarely enough not to become a nuisance. The most old-school ball for this setting is the indoor ball, which is made specifically for a gym-type floor with a soft plastic shell and rather large holes. These features result in greater drag and spin resistance and drastically slow down the pace of play. This type of Open Play is thus more popular with older folk and non-tennis players, with many higher-level players outright refusing to partake. The gym floor may also have a shiny glare or crisscrossing non-pickleball lines, which can be distracting enough to dissuade some from playing.

The more modern form of Open Play now occurs on permanent pickleball courts with an asphalt/acrylic surface similar to tennis courts or on tennis courts lined for pickleball. Many tennis clubs have responded to the rising demand by surfacing new pickleball courts or by fitting two to four pickleball courts on one tennis court with temporary nets and lines. Pickleball-only facilities have been and continue to be built at a rapid rate as well. The balls most often used for this type of Open Play are harder and have relatively small holes, causing them to fly faster and spin more but also to break more often.[2] Nearly all tournaments use these kinds of balls, which means more serious players tend to attend these Open Play sessions, if they do at all.

In all cases, Open Play offers the same mix of personalities and the same feelings of community mentioned previously, though the social dynamics can sometimes require rather

---

2. The market for pickleballs has been flooded with brands in recent years, though the industry standards that the rest are still compared to are Dura and Franklin. Franklin balls are a little softer and don't seem to break as much. Relatedly, I find it problematic that Dura sells a ball that is not very "dura-ble." The amount of plastic that goes straight to the landfill is one of the darker sides of pickleball. Every time a ball breaks, I hurt a little inside.

The underlying cause in scenarios where ego and mastery goals sour the experience seems to be a player's relationship with tournaments. The win-at-all-costs Open Play player is less likely to compete in tournaments regularly. Thus, Open Play essentially becomes "their tournament," to quote several interviewees. On the contrary, the improve-at-all-costs player is more likely to compete in tournaments and thus treats Open Play as an opportunity to better prepare themselves. There is also a third category, the "no tournament" player, who has goals, perhaps temporarily, that are completely divorced from the competition and can also lead to conflict. Suzy Q describes a situation like this, where she was pushed to adjust her goals due to being isolated:

> *"One time I made [my partner] really, really mad. We were playing [in Open Play], and they set it up so that you get one partner and you stay with that partner the whole day. It was just a fun round-robin thing. So, I get [a lower-level male acquaintance]. We play the first game, and we get destroyed—they just picked on him the whole time. I'm like, 'All right, I wanna hit the ball,' so I started playing left-handed, and we lost. And he was so mad at me . . . He was like, 'That's so disrespectful! You're disrespecting them!' And I said, 'Hey, guess what, they hit me the ball. They hit me the ball a lot.' And you know what? I probably still played better than he did! Even though I played left-handed . . . He was so mad he was screaming at me. That was a big ordeal."*

In this case, Suzy Q's actions were interpreted as insufficiently competitive and, therefore, disrespectful to her opponents. There is, of course, the very real possibility that her partner overreacted, but the important point is that goals need to be properly aligned for a harmonious, coopetive experience. There is no inherent issue with someone playing silly, for example, as long as there is some sort of "working consensus"[XL] that silliness is the appropriate mood of the hour. Finding that working consensus in pickleball can be a delicate process.

Another potential source of conflict regarding Open Play does not really concern the players at all, but instead, the *non-players* in the immediate surroundings. The sound of a pickleball striking a paddle is a conspicuously loud *pop*, which is especially noticeable against a quiet backdrop. Pickleball also tends toward longer rallies and longer durations of play times compared with other racquet sports, so the *popping* can be both persistent and prolonged. In large group situations where there are multiple courts having long rallies over several hours, this can create a bona fide chorus of *pops*, like kernels on a kettle. Predictably, the noisiness has been the object of many complaints in many communities across the US, with some actually issuing bans on the sport.[XLI] For many individuals who oppose the sport's sudden ubiquity, the noise issue seems to be at the center of their displeasure.[6]

Pickleballers are well habituated to the noise, however, as it often recedes into the background like a soundtrack in an elevator. Some players absolutely *love* pickleball noise, with Suzy Q, for instance, claiming it to be "music to [her] ears." Many others enjoy its familiarity and the anticipation it builds as one approaches courts with players already playing. Personally, I equate pickleball noise with *mirth* and take it as a signal that people are having a good time nearby. When I hear the *pop*

---

6. I have heard some critics go so far as to call pickleball a "cult" and its players "pests."

sound, it's like my insides perk up and start to smile. Usually, I hear actual laughter not long after, too. It is also not universal that non-players dislike the noise. I was surprised by two of my roommates once at a tournament when they both commented on how they found the incessant *popping* to be soothing, with one actually claiming they could sleep to it.

Despite all that has been said about the conflicts that can arise in Open Play, I tend to agree with an assessment made by Air Pickleball and Rowdy Ria that, for the most part, things are "positive" and that "there's always a one percent." Indeed, Open Play environments are generally quite fun, and the good moments vastly outnumber the bad. In my experience, even the tantrums and pouty behavior common to all sports seem to be kept to a minimum by the strength of pickleball's sociality. Noise complaints, too, are quite rare in the grand scheme of things.

8

PRIVATE GROUPS

IT IS A CHILLY, blustery afternoon in late October when dusk starts to fall and the park's court lights start to glow. All six courts are filled with players, though my attention is on Juke, the player across from me in skinny singles. I have won two closely contested games, but Juke's freshness starts to wane and I am up big in the third game, 6-1. I catch my mind starting to wander in subconscious response to our gap in ability. I try to remind myself to stay focused and to bring my best, and I do.

Backhand chip, volley, volley, smash! My serve.

I pummel the serve, then lag to his return and sloppily miss a forehand wide. Rats. Okay, new strategy. Imagine there is a pretty girl watching, someone you want to impress.

Good! It works. My serve again. I'm locked in, and I win two more points to go up 8-1. On the next point, I drop the ball in the kitchen and come in, then dink, dink, speed up! Juke reflects the ball back, high to my forehand volley, but I hesitate, just for a millisecond, and my muscles drag. I don't crush it quite like I should. He then makes a good reflex, and I dump the next volley into the net. Ugh. I feel lackluster but also queerly content with losing points to even the play. It's almost like self-sabotage. My best game lies dormant and out of my reach, somewhere deep within me. I win the game mostly going through the motions, 11-7.

We switch sides, and Juke proposes a new setup, one where I have to cover the full court and he only has to cover half so that I "get something out of it." We play the first point, and I zig and zag to balls before missing badly. Woah, this is tough! There are no holes, no gaps, and I am run ragged. It feels like I'm playing Ben Johns on steroids.[1] My brow furrows, and I feel a slight tightening in my stomach. The whole world narrows to just the task at hand. Nothing else matters except the next shot, the next breath. My synapses are firing, and my best game suddenly leaps onto the court like a puma onto its prey. I feel actual improvement from one point to the next. Nevertheless, I lose the game. In fact, I never had much chance, and now it's Juke who is lagging, even hitting out-balls[2] to even the field.

I tell him we'll go again, and this time, "My level is going to rise."

---

1. Ben Johns is the most popular choice for #1 overall player as of this writing.
2. "Out-balls" are balls that are going out but have not yet hit the ground. Having a keen eye for these is a legitimate skill since, by hitting them, a player sacrifices an opportunity to win the point.

He laughs and says, "Yeah, cuz' it *has* to!"

I get back into full focus but again fall into a deficit. We play a long point, and I anticipate and cut to balls with the sharpness of a katana. No delay. Then, I black out and retrieve a shot for a down-the-line winner that causes Juke to start exclaiming in awe midway. I even surprise myself; I didn't know I could do that!

I take a breather by the fence and snap out of my stupor for a moment. The wind howls, and a ball from another court rolls near my feet. I tap the ball to a girl who comes to get it, and I'm struck with a curious inspiration. I ask her, "Hey, um, if I may ask, it's cold, dark, windy, kinda late at night . . . Why on earth are you here right now, playing pickleball?"

She smiles and says that she just moved from Minnesota a month ago. She was introduced to pickleball through the fitness club, and now she's addicted. "I'm here because it's fun! Why are *you* here?"

* * *

In addition to pick-up and Open Play, the final practice setup that commonly occurs is a privately organized group consisting of two or more players. Sessions last anywhere from one to five hours and ordinarily feature one to four courts playing doubles and/or mixed doubles, though singles and skinny singles are arranged as well, especially among higher-level players. Most of the venues for these get-togethers are no different than pick-up or Open Play, but a select few are among the coziest in pickleball, as I have been fortunate enough to be invited to several backyards, four pickleball "barns," and an indoor court in a business park.

In a sense, private groups work against the collective spirit of pickleball since they have the downside of being exclusive to only those invited. Though pickleballers are often seasoned adults, this can lead to social tension and hurt feelings, with some describing the petty drama as "like middle school." There can also be some awkward moments when a private group is organized in a location traditionally used for pick-up or Open Play. In one case, my group of high-level players was at a public park, and while taking a break between games, an older gentleman walked onto our court and called out, "We need two!" indicating that he and a friend were looking for two of us to join them for a pick-up game. We then apologetically explained that we organized our group to play only among ourselves.

Of course, the primary virtue of private groups is that one's opponents can be neatly controlled. Apart from the obvious social benefit of being around people one presumably enjoys, this means that skill levels can be matched more or less evenly. If my journey through pickleball has taught me anything, it is this: the best thing that can happen to a pickleball player, or indeed, any athlete, is to be opposed by an opponent who is at or just above their skill level, with the former being the best for the *pair*. Who wins or loses, or even at what level the players compete, whether it's beginner or pro, pales in comparison.

This observation is certainly not new, as coaches, players, and even academics have come to the same conclusion for a very long time. Over sixty years ago, in his influential book *Man, Play and Games*, Roger Caillois argued that a game or sport becomes no longer pleasing for the individual who "wins effortlessly and infallibly" and that "the search for equality is so obviously essential to the rivalry that it is re-established by a handicap for players of different classes."[XLII] Such a "handicap" could be something physical, like added weight, but it could also be abstract, like the rule change in my practice with Juke that gave me extra court to cover. The observation has also been made in sport settings as far away from the pickleball court as can be imagined, such as in the boxing gym. Loïc Wacquant argues that "everything hinges" on the choice of a sparring partner with the goal to "maintain equilibrium" so that both fighters benefit and the risk of injury is minimized, even handicapping one fighter if need be.[XLIII]

Pickleball is no different from boxing in this regard, and I would go so far as to say that equality of opponents is at the very heart of coopetition and, therefore, at the heart of all sports. The potential or the "best" within a player is simply an abstraction until an opponent of matching ability brings it out of them.[3] It cannot be done by the strength of will of a player alone. What's more, there is what I call a "magic hand," like that of a puppeteer, that causes opponents' performance levels to magnetize and approach each other.[4] I believe this "magic hand" to be the mechanism that is behind momentum swings and the phenomenon so frequently heard from athletes who claim that they play "up" or "down" to their opponents.

---

3. This is slightly different from saying that competition, in general, raises one's level, though that is often true as well. As Mr. Keating says in *Dead Poets Society*, "Sports are a chance for us to make other human beings push us to excel," though my point is that a Newtonian equal-and-opposite opponent (or one just better) does this best.

4. Agassi refers to a "magnetic force" pulling him toward the finish line of a competition and an "other force" pushing him away.[XLIV] I argue these are the same force, the force of coopetition, which I refer to here as the "magic hand."

One effect of having the equality of opponents established in private groups is that the points are better. Neither side is overwhelmed by the other nor able to effortlessly punish the other, allowing for a great degree of what the philosopher Hans-Georg Gadamer calls "leeway," or creative response to others' movement.[XLV] Because the court is small, the net is high, and the ball is relatively slow and does not bounce much, there is a back-and-forth of rallies in pickleball that can extend to epic proportions, especially between equals. Players cannot easily hit balls out of reach of their opponents nor smash their way to victory, so they must get creative. The tension that then builds in these rallies, which in doubles often includes a host of very lightly tapped dinks, may go unobserved by the bored non-player but reaches a very satisfying release for the players and educated observers involved.

In a word, pickleball rallies are fun. M1 briefly reflects on this:

"You get some crazy gets[5] all the time in pickleball, you know what I mean? The points extend, and it's just so much fun."

Thus, we arrive at the third cornerstone of pickleball, in addition to competition and community: players consider the game to be *fun*. This may seem cliché—after all, aren't all sports supposed to be fun?—but I assure you, dear reader, that something different is going on here. The fun factor has never been commented on so frequently and so profusely in all my dabbling in sports. It is not that pickleball is more fun, necessarily, than other sports; it is that the fun is an especially

---

5. A "get" simply refers to a retrieved ball, though it is usually used when there is a perceived difficulty in retrieving said ball.

salient feature of the sport and for a very large proportion of its participants.[XLVI] In Wakka's case, the intensity of the fun, in combination with pickleball's other virtues, has completely won him over:

> *"I told my wife the other day, if I die on the pickleball court, just know, that I died happy. I died doing something I love, so I just want you to know, that if I die on the pickleball court, just say that you know I died doing what I love [all said half in laughter]. And I do mean it. It is that cool."*

Partly, the fun comes from the lesser physical strain required to play (in doubles), which leads to players playing and playing and playing as their bodies' natural "limit" takes longer to reach. The fun just doesn't seem to stop. Here is an exchange with M1 that illustrates this point:

> *M1: To me, [pickleball is] never enough. That's what's so weird about it. I never feel like I'm getting enough. I just always wanna keep doing it. [laughter]*
>
> *Me: Pickleball is hypnotic in that way. You feel like you can go forever.*
>
> *M1: It's weird. It's weird how satisfying it is to hit that silly little wiffleball. [laughter]*

To some extent, the fun is *hard* to stop, considering the addictive quality of the sport. While it is true that pickleballers may find themselves playing all the time, which could be a problem in its own right, it is also true that within a single session, pickleballers may find themselves like the compulsive gambler at the roulette wheel, unwilling or unable to walk away.

Private groups especially have a tendency to play three-plus hours or overstay their welcome. "Let's play one more" is a phrase I have heard thousands of times over, and oftentimes, the general attitude of the group is "Let's just play until they kick us out." This can lead to conflict in settings like tennis clubs. In one case at a tennis club, my group played "one more" about four times and stayed thirty minutes past time, while the less-laissez-faire-with-time-slots tennis player in me started to feel very uncomfortable. In a different case, my group stayed only about five minutes over time but faced the wrath of a very ornery tennis coach who complained (probably rightfully) that pickleball players "always" disrespect others' court time.[6]

Another effect of the "fun-diction" of pickleball is that players are often willing to push through pain to continue playing and/or unwilling to take the necessary time off to heal from injury. Partly, this is because players can compete decently well despite lingering ailments, which is again a function of the sport not being the most physically demanding. Many players feel that if they can still play at all, the gains outweigh the pains.

Nuke, for instance, receives cortisone injections for chronic knee pain every four months or so, yet has embraced the challenge, citing the "blessing" that pickleball has been for him "in so many ways." The connection between pain management strategies and enjoyment was made more explicit, however, by Rosey in a practice in which his back locked up on him several times. After insistently urging him to take a break, not just for

---

6. This is also reflective of a "culture war" between tennis and pickleball, as tennis players can be very jealous and dismissive of the game they indirectly helped spawn. Wakka relates it to his experience with snowboarding when it started to encroach on skiing in the 1990s.

the moment but also for the longer time necessary to allow himself to heal, Rosey indicated to me that he could not stop because "pickleball's just too much fun."

Despite all this, only someone with a Scrooge-like sensibility could say that the fun element of pickleball is predominantly a negative thing. Perhaps pickleball's fun-diction causes some undesirable side effects from time to time, but more numerous and important are the mountains of enjoyable experiences had by pickleballers on a daily basis, many of which are produced in privately organized groups. The connections between the members of these groups, mediated by the fun of pickleball, solidify over time and have the capacity to produce lifelong friendships.

One last observation related to the fun of pickleball that, admittedly, I have only circumstantial evidence for is that the social world created in and around pickleball,[7] in my experience, seems to arouse a positive orientation of the spirit toward fellow human beings, even *off* the court, post-play. I have noticed this in an innumerable number of minute interactions in pickleball that are difficult to depict, but two specific anecdotes stand out. After Condor, Juke, and I finished the practice described in the vignette for Chapter VI ("Pick-up Games"), Juke's dad, whom we had also included in our hits, spontaneously purchased the Subway sandwich of a young woman who had inadvertently lined up in the middle of us. The heartwarming moment had the feel of a man who felt cheerful from his life's events for the day and then felt motivated to spread such cheer to a stranger.

---

7. In the 1930s, Dutch theorist Johan Huizinga coined the term "magic circle" to describe the separate and defined space of play and games, where the rules create and allow for a certain kind of social world.[XLVII] This seems particularly apt for pickleball—there's some magic there.

On a separate occasion, Juke and I were approached by a homeless man while eating lunch at a park in St. Louis after finishing several hours of pickleball. The man was searching for a cigarette, which we did not have, and then stayed for some friendly conversation. After some time, Juke told the man he might have something for him after all and started to his car, at which point a homeless woman who had kept to herself a short distance away spoke up, telling us that she too could use some help. Juke returned from his car and gave each of them twenty dollars, and we chatted with the woman for another twenty minutes. I felt so touched and inspired by this act of kindness that the next day, when a fellow graduate student came to me asking for donations to help a struggling immigrant family who had been rudely bussed to town by Texas Governor Greg Abbott, I knew exactly where my remaining one hundred dollars of recent pickleball winnings was supposed to go.

Whether pickleball actually promotes a chain reaction of prosocial acts or not, it certainly *feels* like it does. Regardless, the sociality and fun that come from pickleball *are* real, and they really contribute to a coopetive sporting atmosphere. Neither the community nor the fun is contingent on specific outcomes of play, though winning is certainly felt more positively than losing. It is now time to turn to more competitive settings to see if or how these things change, in addition to pickleballers' perceptions of success.

9

LOW-STAKES COMPETITIONS

FOUR HOURS INTO A PRIVATELY organized money tournament of twenty-eight teams, The Flash and I are opposed in the semifinals by two of our good friends. The two of them are fresh off an intense quarterfinal match, surviving a comeback bid from a duo of pesky pickleball YouTubers. All eyes now shift to our match, including those of our informal videographers and biggest fans, Rowdy Ria and Air Pickleball. Anticipation builds and is only interrupted by the shooting of an occasional plume of hot air through the tarped ceiling, similar to Sonic the Hedgehog through a chute.

Due to the respect we have for the matchup, we manage to convince the organizer to let us play a full two out of three games to eleven instead of the planned one game to fifteen. Play starts, and The Flash and I race to an 11-1, 5-0 lead as our friends rather disappointingly come out flat. To their credit, they do raise their game and challenge us the rest of the way, including a wild point in which one of them scrambles back from the sideline to hit a laser volley between the two of us for a winner. Finally, at 10-9-2,[1] I whack a serve very near the line in the deep corner that is returned long. Our friends suspect the serve was out but cannot completely agree, thus giving us the victory. The crowd applauds, and we tap paddles.

Approximately a minute later, as we are on the sideline, I catch wind from some observers that my last serve was indeed out. I turn to our friends and ask them if they would like to replay the point, to which they eagerly agree, as does The Flash. The four of us then retake our positions to an applause considerably louder than when the match first "ended." It seems the crowd appreciates the good sportsmanship and an opportunity to watch more pickleball. We proceed to *lose* the point and the next point, which ties the game at 10-10 and breathes new life into the competition. I worry that if our friends turn the tables and win the match, I will be responsible for my partner receiving less prize money. Luckily for us, we push through some tough points and win the game, 12-10. The crowd applauds for the second time, and our friends are much more at ease to have lost in less ambiguous circumstances.

---

1. Since both players on a team serve, the "2" here just means "second server." Losing the point then gives the serve back to the other team (called a "side out"), who would call the score "9-10-1," since the server's score is called first and they would be on their first server.

Months later, I happen to observe a very similar situation in an informal prize money tournament run by my friends, the Zero-Zero's. A ball is called out to end the tournament, the players tap paddles, and then begin to walk off. Murmurings among the audience that the ball was actually in then prompt the player who called the ball out to propose to replay the last point. The audience claps, and the players retake their positions. This time, however, the team given new life actually *wins* the second game, then wins the third game, the match, and the top prize. It is a small loss for the team who proposed to continue the match but a big win for pickleball and for all who are there. I go home happy, despite the fact that my team lost before the finals.

* * *

Like all sports, tournaments offer a stage for pickleballers to test their skills with elevated stakes. The majority of such tournaments draw locally, most often to a park, gymnasium, tennis club, or pickleball club, and the stakes are relatively low. Many are actually informal and privately organized, sometimes even in one's backyard, and can involve small sums of money to be won by the highest performers. Despite the direct competition and occasional cash prizes, however, the coopetive spirit of pickleball is on display at these events in a variety of ways.

For starters, the nature of how pickleball winners are identified, honored, and referred to has a coopetive bent. Pickleball uses an Olympic-style system of gold, silver, and bronze, each with a corresponding medal, and each listed online if the tournament is formal enough. Players will often refer to their performance by whether or not they "medaled" or may refer to the specific medal, such as "I got bronze." This extension of accolades beyond solely first place allows for a wider range of players to experience formal recognition for their performance. The quip that "nobody remembers second place," though speaking truth in so many sports that I have experienced, applies much less in pickleball.

Next, pickleball tends to be coopetive even in the basic structure of its tournaments, as the most popular formats include the round-robin format and the double-elimination format. "Round robin" is a general sports term that refers to cycling through each and every opponent so that everyone plays everyone. What's more, each individual match of the round robin is usually truncated to a single game, either to eleven or fifteen, which contributes to a sense that "anybody can beat anybody" since upsets occur more easily in shorter time frames. For some tournaments, winners are decided by those with the most victories or the most points, though in others, the best performers from the round-robin advance to a knockout stage and winners are determined like a traditional tournament.[2]

The second popular format, double-elimination, is somewhat of a rarity in competitive sports. In this format, players are arranged like a typical tournament, though after a loss, players drop into a back draw and must lose a second time to actually be eliminated. This means that a player can lose but then proceed through the back draw to reach the

---

2. In larger tournaments, participants may be put into groups, with the round-robin proceeding within each group. Top performers then advance to a knockout stage so that the groups are integrated.

championship, where usually they must win back-to-back matches to be named the champion. Unlike most sports, which, using a more traditional tournament format, demand that their champions have a perfect record, double-elimination pickleball allows its champions to possibly be humbled along the way. This extends hope and motivation to a great many who have stumbled in the early goings. Oftentimes, after completing a main draw match, I have told my opponents, "Hope to see you later in the tournament," or something similar, which lends support to them and the idea of a possible rematch.

Scoring is another element of pickleball with a coopetive edge, particularly in doubles. The system can appear convoluted for amateurs, and even with the score customarily being called out before each serve, it is very common for both amateurs and experienced players to momentarily forget or get confused about the score, who should be serving, or where everyone should be positioned.[3] On numerous occasions in lower-stakes events with no referee present, I have seen the score become a cooperative endeavor, not just to keep track of but also to confirm whether the current setup or positioning of players was right or wrong. There is occasional flexibility in the score, too, such as in the introduction to this chapter, where scoring parameters may be negotiated, mistakes may be corrected, and/or points may be re-done. For comparison, the handshake in tennis is such a sacred act

---

3. Several memes, bumper stickers, sweatshirts, and t-shirts play up the score confusion, with my favorite being, "Who's serve? What's the score? What day is it? Who are you people?"

for ending a match that I have never seen players ever recon-vene to continue playing.[4] It is even difficult to imagine.

On the topic of ending matches, the customary way to end a pickleball match is for all players to approach the net and lightly tap each other's paddle. This extends to all games of any finality, including those in rec play. It is also quite common for players to do some form of paddle tapping when switching sides of the court, especially when one game of a two-out-of-three match has finished. This friendly gesture is so ingrained in pickleball that professional Riley Newman made quite a stir on May 31, 2023, when he declared on Instagram:

> *"After much thought, consideration and admiration for the great game of pickleball, I have personally decided that going forward I will forgo the tapping of paddles after each game. I know this will be off-putting to some but I believe this will help elevate the optics of pro pickleball. In addition to that, I also think it's a silly thing to do. In no other sport do you see opponents come together in the middle of competition and say 'good job.' They wait until competition is over to do that—which is exactly what I will be doing as well."*[XLIX]

The general looseness in format and scoring in non-professional pickleball tournaments and the minor uproar caused by Newman's declaration are tangential to the fourth and final pillar of pickleball; in addition to competition, com-munity, and fun, there is *playfulness*. Pickleball is playful at its roots, and this plays out even at higher stakes. Nicknames (dis-cussed on page 35) are an obvious example, as players have

---

4. The only time I have heard of an instance where an official competition was reconvened due to a missed call after a ritual conclusion was Minnesota State versus Bemidji State in hockey in 2022. The event was rare enough to be featured in a breakdown by Jomboy Media.[XLVIII]

traditionally been able to choose to compete with a stage name instead of their real name. One local tournament I participated in played up on this, labeling its highest competition level the "LEGENDS" division and giving each player a fancy nickname. Appearances are another example. One team at a different local tournament sported beards on just half of their faces so that they were comical mirror images of each other, with one of the players also deliberately wielding an archaic wooden paddle. Relatedly, consider this exchange with Ping Pong Mike:

> *Ping Pong Mike: I go to tournaments, and I said to myself, first and foremost, I wanna have fun. So, I bought uniforms.*
>
> *Me: What do you mean? For yourself?*
>
> *Ping Pong Mike: Yeah, for pickleball tournaments.*
>
> *[shows me photos of wild pickleball jerseys for himself and his partners, including designs with dragons, kitties, and Power Rangers.]*
>
> *Me: So, you like dragons?*
>
> *Ping Pong Mike: No. I don't like them; I find them ugly as hell. I just find the ugliest shirts I can and put my partners in them. Because it's funny as hell. [laughter]*

Indeed, Ping Pong Mike and I later teamed up to win gold at two separate events wearing flaming wolf muscle shirts and mystic dragon T-shirts, respectively. I have also worn playfully themed uniforms in two team events run by Minor League Pickleball (MiLP). Recruited by my friends, the Zero-Zero's, our team competed at MiLP's "DUPR 20 Nationals"[5] event

---

5. Minor League Pickleball events limit teams to four players whose DUPR ratings collectively add up to a number less than the stated number, such as 16, 18, 20, etc.

in Orange County as the "Mutant Ninja Pickles," and did so wearing matching shirts, hats, and socks featuring the Teenage Mutant Ninja Turtles. (I was the purple one, Donatello.) The event even included a cash prize of $1,000 for the uniforms voted to be the best on social media, which we lost to a team with colorful wigs and long stockings. Then, weeks later, with a slightly altered lineup, our team competed at a local DUPR 20 event as the "Picklets," featuring cute pig faces on our shirts.

To be clear, though, the majority of players do not engage in these methods of outright playfulness. Instead, what's interesting is that the spirit of pickleball is playful enough not only to allow these things but also to keep them from being out of place. The outwardly playful minority are also not un-serious players; on the contrary, these players are often avid competitors. Pickleball simply allows for multiple expressions of the human character to be on display.

Theoretically, this ensures that teams are evenly matched, though teams try to game the system with newer players that are not appropriately rated yet. The motivation for this, beyond the simple desire to win, is that there is usually a cash prize.

Further, pickleball tournaments are permeated with a friendly playfulness in subtle ways that are difficult to capture. Compliments are shared between teams for quality shots at a high rate. Jokes are common. Players sometimes actively call their own shots out or help their opponents make calls. Random players sometimes volunteer or are called upon to act as warm-up partners. Audience members occasionally become brief, mid-match discussion partners. I once heard an opening server of a high-stakes match pause before serving and say, "Let's have a fun and fair match!" I witnessed a player be positively bamboozled by a spin serve,[6] react with a grin and remark how "silly" he looked, then collaborate with his opponent after the match on how to hit or approach such a shot. One time, an opponent asked me to play more on the same court even after our match had concluded. At a different time, an opponent voluntarily defaulted to me after I had built a sizable lead but faced a time crunch to leave the event.

All of these observations point to an overarching prosocial, playful disposition in pickleball despite its competitive seriousness. There are adults hard at work, grinding toward victory, but there are also inner children, so to speak, joyfully and spontaneously improvising.[L] To further highlight this, M1 describes one of his recent tournament experiences:

---

6. "Spin serves" are when the server uses either their paddle or their opposite hand to spin the ball on the toss to serve. If done correctly, the served ball will take a wicked bounce on the opponent's side. The former method, called the "chainsaw" serve, was banned in most official tournaments at the end of 2021 because its effect was too intense. The latter method, which is milder in effect, was tolerated for an extra year but then banned as well at the end of 2022.

"Part of what's so fun about [tournaments] is people are watching, and I'm talking to people who are watching . . . In [a recent] tournament I had a couple friends who were there, and I was just talking to them during the matches. Not about the match, just about whatever . . . It just was more relaxed, having fun, and any time I start to get nervous, I turn around and I say, 'Start smiling,' and I start to smile. 'Here, this is pickleball! Smile at that ball that's coming at you!' I might look a little crazy, but I put on a smile, and it's just like, 'Here we go; it's fun!' [said clownishly]"

To be clear, M1 desires very much to play well and to win, but the somewhat paradoxical lightheartedness of pickleball tournaments is ever present and steers him (and others) away from approaching the task with the life-and-death seriousness sometimes seen in other sports. It should also be noted that pickleball tournaments are total events that include not just play but also travel, communion, and social gathering. Sometimes, this is even experienced as a pause or break from real life. As such, if one does not perform to their liking, there are often many other opportunities to take home a positive experience. Several interviewees comment on the pleasure of the overall tournament experience, including Ping Pong Mike:

"My favorite thing about pickleball—it's fifty-fifty. I love the game. I also love traveling to tournaments, and going to dinner afterward, and just talking shit about whoever. It's like high school . . . The socializing aspect is [often] more fun than the tournament."

On some level, tournaments are experienced this way simply because a group of like-minded individuals engage in a shared activity. Still, I suspect pickleball's playfulness has something to do with it. Ping Pong Mike is one of many to compare pickleball to a time when most adults enjoyed a more playful existence, such as early education. The "fountain of youth" is another common metaphor applied to pickleball, which also harkens back to earlier times.

It must be stressed, however, that many of these elements of playfulness are only truly characteristic of local, privately organized, and other low-stakes competitions. In professional or high-prestige events, the playful element predictably wanes, though it never disappears entirely. It is remarkable that it exists as it does at any level of competition. Wordsmith Ping Pong Mike makes sense of this rather brilliantly, claiming that at pickleball's roots, "It's a fucking wiffleball out there with paddles, and we're all dicking around." That it is, and that we are.

10

HIGH-STAKES COMPETITIONS

IT'S EARLY IN THE MORNING on New Year's Day when I wake up in a motel four hours earlier than I would normally prefer. Over the past two days, I completed singles and doubles at a regional tournament hosted in an indoor tennis center. Now, I await an impromptu pairing with Suzy Q in mixed doubles, which will be my first mixed tournament in several years. I did not expect or intend to play, but when duty calls to fill in as a substitute partner after Juke tweaks a muscle, *c'est la vie*. There are certainly worse things than an extra dose of pickleball.

Thus far, aside from Juke's injury, the weekend has been very successful. Juke and I met our goal of a gold medal showing in doubles, and singles was a good time, too, including the best point I have ever been a part of and lost. More importantly, I felt like I was in the process of high-intensity improvement and competition while also developing new friends and relationships. Fun was had off the court as well, featuring an excellent Spanish refresher in a long chat with a Colombian family in the hotel hot tub, in addition to a festive dinner at The Cheesecake Factory courtesy of Juke and his girlfriend.

After a twenty-five-minute drive, I arrive at the venue feeling a little fatigued and low on fluids. This does not concern me, however, as my general disposition toward mixed doubles could be described as ambivalent at best. Twenty years of tennis have prejudiced me against it, as I don't enjoy the general strategy of targeting the woman and preying on the physical performance gap. I also don't enjoy "stealing" my partner's balls by taking three-quarters of the court to try to win. For these reasons, tennis mixed doubles was mostly just an opportunity to flirt with my partner in the past. For pickleball, I know the performance gap is not as large, I know most women *want* the guy to take most of the court, and I know my attitude generally needs a makeover, but no matter what I tell myself, I'm really just hoping to put in a good showing and go home.

Suzy Q has different ideas. When I find her, she says she arrived a full forty minutes before I did out of nervousness and worry that something might go wrong. She's clearly excited and very invested in the result. The tournament means a lot to her, as it is an opportunity to play with an unusually talented partner and to put her name on the map for top women's players in the region. When I voice my honest concerns about my own biases, she reiterates her desire to win and assures me that taking the majority of the court is not a bother for her; in fact, she actually expects it. I wrestle with conflicting thoughts as we warm up, work on some shots, and discuss strategy.

In our first match, neither of our opponents plays well, and we win comfortably. Nevertheless, the match is largely an exercise in me *not* learning my lesson. Though Suzy Q and I do decide to stack,[1] strategically and positionally, I play more or less like it is regular doubles. With cognitive dissonance fluttering in my mind, indecision, lapses in judgment, and semi-involuntary muscle relaxations lead to mistakes that were absent from my performance the day before. Our male opponent, a new friend who I played in the men's doubles, jokingly remarks that I "finally missed one" and eventually that I missed "more than all of yesterday." There is a huge highlight, however, as Suzy Q defends several shots hit like missiles before sending back an audacious missile of her own that squeaks by our male opponent, to the surprise of everybody. This elicits a raucous "WOOO!!" in the classic arms-to-the-sky Rocky pose from a self-amazed Suzy Q.

In our second match, we match up against another one of my relatively new friends, who is also one of my favorite players to play. He sports a competitive yet delightfully playful spirit

---

1. "Stacking" is when a doubles team takes advantage of the court's smaller proportions to arrange players according to their greatest perceived strength. In practice, this means that before the point, two players may stand on the same side, or one player may stand off the court to the side. Once the serve (or return) is struck, players then shift a few steps to fulfill the desired arrangement. In our case, this ensured that the stronger player (me) always played on the left side so that my right-handed forehand (and strongest shot) was always in the middle. Stacking is now how nearly every high-level team plays, with many players training to perform only on a specific side of the court.

that is perfect for pickleball. Though I have bested him in the past, he shows me a new side to him in this match, the "alpha" side, which comes out for some male (and occasionally female) players in mixed doubles who really embrace the role of team leader.[2] This is the best I've seen him play, and frankly, we fail to match his team's intensity. "We" in this case means me, as I again suffer from some of the issues in the previous match. I try hard, though, and both games are long, extended dances in the early going, with one extremely long rally that is interrupted by a ball from a neighbor court standing out as a turning point in the first game.[3] Nonetheless, our opponents eventually pull away in both cases for an 11-4, 11-5 victory.

Initially, I feel only minor disappointment, as the result fits my unspoken goal of a "good showing." Suzy Q is distraught, however, and this causes me to re-evaluate. I confess to her that I'm finding it difficult to stay engaged, and by that, I mean to compete with the intensity and purpose that would give our team the best chance to win. Suzy Q basically responds with what I interpret to be her greatest George Costanza impression: "You're not engaged? Well, you better *get* engaged!" This sinks in, and I am finally ready to stop thinking like an individual. Instead, I think, *What is the best our* team *can bring?* If our team's product is mutually constructed, I must also conform to the terms of my partner, and even to some extent, those which are established by our opponents. If everyone else is doing their

---

2. Later, this opponent told me he "likes the strategy [of mixed] better," which I have heard from several male players. Though I still prefer men's doubles, I now enjoy mixed doubles and no longer feel like I did at the time of this experience. I suspect my older views were ethnocentric, possibly even chauvinistic.
3. I have to fight very hard not to call a game a "set," which is the equivalent in tennis.

level best to win, and I am making an effort but not in a way that takes winning seriously enough, I am being somewhat of a spoilsport.

With a new mindset in place, Suzy Q and I cruise through the draw. It's coopetition in high gear. I start flying around the court, encroaching often on her side, and both of us start to play much better. In one match, I miss only a single shot. In a rematch versus the team who beat us, we win both games, though we face a game point down in the second game.[4] For the final, we must defeat the team once in a full match and once again in a tiebreaking game to fifteen. Our opponents play well, but Suzy Q shines, especially after gaining full confidence in dink rallies versus the female player. We again escape from a game point down in the first game, and then the hope and life of the opposing team gradually start to fade. Our effort proves good enough for the gold medal.

Though the crowd mostly supports our opponents, who happen to be a local team, everyone is very complimentary and congratulatory afterward. I even get a text from The Mayor, who is several states away. My friend who first defeated us amusingly yet pointedly tells me not to bring my "pro ass" back. The director of the tournament gives a colorful speech at the medal ceremony in front of an impressively large podium. (Snippet: "By the power vested in me, I bestow upon you this medal and all that goes along with it . . . which *ain't much*.")

---

4. Interestingly, the first game in this match was extremely tight, possibly the best of the tournament, yet ended 11-5. In the second game, our team had an 8-0 lead that fizzled away somewhat sloppily, leading to a 13-11 finish. This is an excellent example of how a score can *lie*. The first game was much "closer" and featured much better play than the second game.

Overall, there's a feeling that the bustling chaos of the tournament has dissipated and what is left is the feeling of community: cheerful and warm despite some competitive disappointment and the somewhat chilly environs of the tennis center.

I need not ask Suzy Q whether she is satisfied with the result; that much is obvious. However, when we chat hours later at an Italian restaurant, she tells me it was likely the very best moment in her sporting career, which includes quite a bit of participation in high school and college sports. It takes a while for the reality of this to sink in . . . just *wow*. Thank heavens I got over myself.

* * *

Pickleball tournaments are often abuzz. The bigger the tournament and the larger the pool of players, the more bustling the tournament space becomes, similar to a village supermarket or bazaar. Players are constantly moving around to warm up, compete, regroup, and observe others. The shuffling of feet, *popping* of balls, shrieks of agony, gaggles of laughter, and cheers of excitement all mix together in a cacophony that becomes all the more enjoyable the more one plays. There are secondary activities, too, that may encircle the main action, such as vendors (often tented), concessions, video production, emceeing, and loud music.

It is also true that levels of all kinds are frequently mixed together in the overall playing space, contributing to a feeling of organized chaos. This is the case even at most professional events, as such events host skill and age brackets suitable for anyone who wishes to play. Courts are generally packed, and there is very little downtime or absence of action. Plus, who is competing and on which court is often poorly marked, if at all, so that uninformed observers absorb drama somewhat at random and from anonymous and highly varied sources. Pros, skilled amateurs, and near-beginners often share the same walkways, the same locker rooms, and the same courts, though exceptions include grandstands and pro-only lounges, and organizational coherence varies by tournament.[5]

Though many high-stakes draws now span across multiple days, most pickleball tournaments are completed in a single day. This means tournament days can feel really *long* and demand a level of fitness that is not insignificant. Singles is particularly grueling, though brackets are usually bigger in doubles and mixed doubles due to this very fact.[6] For professional draws, singles and doubles brackets are the same size, which means singles champions are nearly always in excellent shape. There is certainly a virtue in testing players to their physical limits, though this setup for singles is borderline dangerous on a hot day, as I have seen top players vomit on court late in a draw. It becomes imperative that players stay hydrated, replenish energy, and use timeouts, of which two are allowed per game.

---

5. As pickleball has grown, professional events have sported less of this melting pot vibe and have approached a clearer division of pros and observers/other players similar to that of tennis, though the mix is still there.

6. Singles and doubles test the body in different ways, but the cardiovascular demands of doubles are noticeably low for an aerobic sport. Players have been shown to take an average of five hundred more steps in singles than in doubles over the course of an hour.[LI] In a personal example, Ping Pong Mike and I played in a doubles tournament versus some of the best players in the world, including JW Johnson, and neither of us ever felt out of breath. The day before, however, Ping Pong Mike found himself lying spread-eagle on the grass because he was huffing and puffing so hard after only a few minutes of one-on-one basketball.

Doubles, though not as physically demanding, requires a great deal of synchronization with one's partner. The choice of partner is almost as important for a player as their performance execution. If a sizable gap in ability exists between partners, higher-level opposing teams are adept at isolating the weaker partner so that a much stronger player can lose to two weaker players playing strategically. Though certainly frustrating, part of the challenge is for teams to maneuver themselves in such a manner that will lead to their best chance of success. This requires effective communication and some degree of compatibility and compromise. Coopetition is thus heavily at work at the partner level, in strategy, in personality, and in movement.

Speaking further on the dynamic of doubles partnership, to some extent, whether or not partners are grooving is *the* barometer of success. In two events with Sharpy, for instance, the two of us struggled to a bronze medal in our first event, sunk to a woeful depth in our second event, and then finally settled on a successful stacking formation at what seemed like the eleventh hour. Though we did not medal in our second event, the feeling that we were finally in sync was immensely satisfying. An effective, coopetive combination of partners can be so satisfying that Bullet claims it might be the highlight of his entire pickleball journey. After two unsuccessful pairings, one of which fizzled due to personality issues and another due to a jealous boyfriend, his pairing with KO became a game-changer. In his words:

> *"I think [my pickleball highlight is] just getting to partner with KO. To see her develop and grow and to have somebody that is a stable partner that is going to grow with me. I don't have to think she's gonna leave to play with somebody else. I know that partnership is*

there. And I know that she's gonna be there every Tuesday, every Wednesday for practice . . . We've just become really good friends. Whether we win or lose, I really don't give a shit. When we go to these tournaments, I think fifty percent of it for me is the drive down, talking, having fun. We talk a ton about pickleball. We do. We talk a ton about shots, strategies, what we need to work on, trying to be positive to each other."

Bullet and KO seem to possess an enviable chemistry, and for as long as it holds, they are a success even before they step on the court. Of course, their pairing is a mixed pairing, which has a flavor that is slightly different from regular doubles. For all intents and purposes, mixed doubles is equally valued by the pickleball community as singles and regular doubles (very unlike tennis). Indeed, professional events award mixed winners equal prize money. Male partners usually commandeer the court, yet it is often the strength of the female partner that is the most crucial predictor of team results, so both have an important role.

There is also a generally accepted notion, akin to folk wisdom, that it is very difficult to compete successfully with one's significant other, with many players pairing with a "pickleball husband" or "pickleball wife." For Maverick, a "really low part" of her pickleball experience is a lack of chemistry with her significant other on the court, though they are not without their good moments. The one couple I interviewed, Air Pickleball and Rowdy Ria, also struggle to play together from time to time. Here is an account of a moment they now laugh about, in Air Pickleball's words:

"We were playing a match, and I saw the ball in. At this time, we were up 7-2 or 7-3, and she called it out. I was like, no honey, it

> *was in. Then she got mad. For the next few points, she just kept hitting the ball out or not trying. She was like, 'I'll show you out!'* "

It is obviously not impossible for significant others to play and get along fine, and there are exceptions, but evidence points to the possibility of there being a slight incongruity in the coopetitive core of pickleball. Couples, even very close friends, for whatever reason, may struggle with teamwork on the court.

The development of ratings has also created a slight incongruity in the coopetive core of pickleball. As players have flooded into the sport, tournament applicants have greatly increased, causing ratings to take on greater importance for qualifying players into draws. DUPR, especially, has become an obsession for some players, as getting drafted onto teams and into leagues largely depends on it, in addition to the general reputational credibility it provides. Unfortunately, though it has undergone several adjustments, DUPR has, at times, penalized players simply for playing other players ranked lower than them. In a personal instance, I was the considerable favorite in a singles event, and though I won without dropping a game, my DUPR actually went *down* by a whopping 0.50 (i.e., almost a full level). As such, one effect of the new ratings dynamic is that skilled players are less keen on playing local events or with less skilled friends and family members just for fun since their rating may be affected. On the other hand, players may also be discouraged from sandbagging and playing below their level, so the effects may balance each other out.

* * *

At this point, despite all that has been said about the dynamics of pickleball that are not strictly competitive, which I have chosen to label as coopetive, there is still a giant elephant in the room. When opponents compete in sport, there are winners and there are losers. Aren't these outcomes mutually exclusive? Isn't that what tournaments, especially high-stakes events, are supposed to be about?

At the risk of stating the obvious, winning takes on greater importance and the atmosphere is less playful at higher-stakes competitions in pickleball. This is a far cry, however, from saying that winning is the only thing that matters for pickleballers. Thus far, this book has attempted to illuminate the coopetitive essence of pickleball and sport to argue against sport as a zero-sum game. (If you remember, dear reader, there is a point to all this beyond just another excuse to talk about pickleball!) We now turn, briefly, to how pickleballers conceive of winning and losing, which is the aspect of sport most closely associated with zero-sum.

First off, it would be wrong to pretend that winning is not on the mind of every single pickleballer who competes in a tournament, almost regardless of the stakes. Winning matters. Nuke estimates its importance for him at "8.5 out of 10," which seems to be not too unusual for a tournament player. Juke, for example, once told me point blank: "I love playing with you because I can *win* with you." The Mayor claims that winning is important because it "validates hard work," and Rowdy Ria has the attitude of "why play" if not to try to win. For many, though certainly not all, winning is attractive because it staves off the torment of losing as well. Thor is in this camp, as he resents the feeling of "not getting over the hump," with losing being something he says he "hates so much." Relatedly, there seems to be a general consensus that it is very difficult to be successful if one is eliminated from a tournament after two losses and no wins (called "going 0-2"), which should be avoided at all costs.

In spite of all this, players' attitudes toward winning seem to be quite malleable, coming with endless caveats, clarifications, and exceptions. To start, only one of my interviewees ever discussed winning as if it is a singular goal, with very little room for seeing success in non-victorious performances. Even in an 0-2 situation, there is the possibility of player success, as M1 recounts a time he went 0-2 yet "had a blast" because of some great points he played with a new partner. On the flip side, "medaling" (i.e., finishing in the top three) is usually indicative of success, but not always. Ping Pong Mike, for instance, once got bronze in a large field yet describes it as his "lowest low" and says he "didn't sleep that night," as he felt he drastically fell short of expectations. Ping Pong Mike is quite positive about a different bronze medal performance, though, because it was "a hell of a field."

What players consider to be successful, therefore, depends on the context, especially the perceived difficulty of the challenge or opponent. If something is perceived as challenging enough, there is really nothing that can't be experienced as a success. Being "pickled," for example, describes an often-embarrassing failure to score a point for an entire game, and yet, Air Pickleball felt "encouraged" by his performance and actually *gained* confidence after I pickled him 11-0 in a game of singles. Likewise, if something is perceived as not challenging enough, even giant victories may feel less than successful. Pickling an opponent is more likely to bring me sadness than joy, which is a sentiment shared by Nuke, who says he "feels bad." In many cases, I would argue that pickling an opponent is actually a failure to find a balanced matchup.

Many of these observations seem to line up with the work of psychologist Mihály Csikszentmihalyi, who claims that our "best moments usually occur when [our] body or mind is stretched to its limits in a voluntary effort to accomplish something difficult and worthwhile."[LII] Indeed, this is likely why the position of the underdog can be such an envious one, such as for Wakka, who claims there is "nothing better" than this kind of winning. In addition, nearly all whom I have interviewed report that their biggest highlight in pickleball stems from a triumph that surprised them or that they had never accomplished before. This is true for Suzy Q, whose ecstasy of accomplishment in this chapter's introduction was doubled due to the teams we defeated being the best she had ever even played before. Consider, too, the pickleball highlight of The Mayor, in which he earned his first silver medal in 4.5:

> *"Not only [did we get the silver medal], but we went to the loser's bracket. We lost the first round and worked all the way back to the championship match . . . We had to beat like nine teams to get back to that spot. We lost the championship, but that was really gratifying. To start from where we were, to lose the first round, not playing together well. Then we just clicked after that first match and ran off like eight in a row to get back to the championship. So that was probably the most gratifying because I'd never had to do that before, and I've never done it again."*

This goes to show that not all wins and losses are created equal. There is also the reality that the value of winning for any player can change rapidly from moment to moment. This has been documented in tennis,[LIII] and pickleball is no different. Critical points, such as being down match point, are experienced closer to zero-sum, in the sense that one side's victory is truly at the *expense* of the other. Points that may tie the score after squandering a large lead are also like this. Other times, players may absorb the goals of their partners, as I did with Suzy Q, or events may trigger spikes in one's desire to win, such as behavior from opponents that is perceived to be dishonest, arrogant, or aggressive. KO describes an instance in which she was rudely body-bagged by her male opponent on the first point of a match,[7] only to then declare "game on" with a burning determination to return the favor to both opponents en route to a victory.

Sometimes, winning may be valued, but something else is valued more and thus is more relevant to a player's success. In many cases, these valuations are mastery goals, such as the majority of those already mentioned. In other cases, what's valued most may have little direct relation with one's performance. Pickle Bella, for instance, often gauges her success on the strength of her sweat at the conclusion of a match or practice session—a method I myself have used on numerous occasions. Similarly, KO's main goal on the court is also one that I identify with:

> *"What's more important to me, more important than winning, is to have really cool points . . . I don't care what the score is . . . I just love the cool points, the cool strategy, and I wanna bring my best*

---

7. A "body bag" (or "peg") refers to a ball that strikes one on the body. These instances are actually pretty well tolerated in pickleball overall, as the ball doesn't hurt *that* much, and players are so close to each other at the kitchen line that body bags are inevitable and part of the game.

to the table. Then, whatever happens, happens, because sometimes, there are really good players that are playing down [in level]. I can't control that for a medal. I'm not gonna go in and say I have to have a silver. I don't have to have that because it's out of my control. If 4.5s are playing down at 4.0, there's nothing I can do about that. If their skill level is beyond me, I'm not gonna look down on myself and say, 'Oh, I didn't get a medal.' I don't go into tournaments for the medal."

KO expresses a coopetive attitude here. "Cool points" require quality play from both sides and nourish the spirit so that there is no loser. On top of that, KO touches on the important fact that winning is most often just not in one's control, which is why it makes little sense for players to take too much stock in a competition's end result. For one, some players have a tendency to register themselves below their rank and play "down" in level so that they can win more easily. This behavior is the subject of much scorn, as it goes against pickleball's coopetive spirit, with Rowdy Ria asking, "Where's the fun in that?"

Randomness is another element that plays a huge role in the outcome of a match and is rarely properly accounted for. The possible pathways of a pickleball match are infinite, and the smallest changes in conditions can have unforeseen effects, just as in life. This aspect of games mimicking life may partly explain why games are so compelling despite the complementary frustration that goes along with built-in chaos. Let courts,[8] for example, are particularly common phenomena in pickleball

---

8. "Let courts" are instances when a ball clips the top of the net and either dribbles over or redirects, giving the receiving player little to no time to properly react.

that cement chaos as an unavoidable feature of the sport. There are thus practical reasons why winning is "not the be all end all," in the words of some of those I have interviewed.

Another factor to consider stems from the fact that most pickleball tournaments are completed on a single day. Tournaments have a set start time, but with no set times after the first round, there is often equal amounts of nervous waiting as there is play. This might mitigate against feeling too strongly about the outcomes of completed matches simply because there is always another match coming. The Mayor compares this with his experience in football:

> *"Pickleball is a sport that you can't really let [the winning/losing feeling] last too long. Because you're right back on the court to do it again. That's the difference versus a football game—the high, you get a whole week or a day or two, but pickleball, you get fifteen minutes, thirty minutes at most, and you're back on the court."*

The takeaway here is that a player cannot afford to ride a win-loss-fueled roller coaster of emotion since new outcomes are soon to come. It is on the process, not the outcomes of performance, ironically, that players must devote most of their attention for their desired outcomes to occur.

In fact, what might be even more important than winning is simply *attempting to win*. This was my main success with Suzy Q, less so the fact that we actually won (though that was nice!). Outside of scenarios in which a certain result may truly be life-changing, or maybe even life-threatening, the outcome of a match is a relatively unimportant by-product compared with the effort that makes it happen, as it is only the overall effort that can be repeated and controlled. For athletes, the golden goose is the act of journeying onward and "taking part"[9] rather than the specific destination.

As discussed earlier, the journey in pickleball happens to be a whole lot of fun, and I suspect this colors the way pickleballers respond to losing matches. At the very least, losing pickleballers who attempted to win and gave their best are still recipients of a good time. Losses, then, come with an opportunity cost in affirmation and possibly in glory but also in fun. A very common refrain from losing pickleballers, for instance, is that they "should have won the last one." Partly, this is a lament that the journey came to an end. An exchange with M1 highlights this:

> *M1: Wins feel good, but you always feel like you gotta get ready for the next one. Losing is, I don't get to play more. That's the frustrating part about losing to me.*
>
> *Me: Sure. Opportunity lost. The fun stops.*
>
> *M1: Opportunity lost, the fun stops . . . that's great. That's exactly the way it feels.*

Losing can also have a shock-to-the-system effect that's similar to being doused by an icy bucket of water. Often, players re-evaluate a perceived failure as a positive learning experience, especially if it proves to be beneficial in the long run. In fact, it seems as though the most obvious of failures are also

---

9. "Taking part" is an Olympic concept that is a vital part of the oath taken by Olympic athletes. Sportswriter Robert Creamer's take on this concept reflects my thinking here: "The often-misunderstood Olympic concept of 'taking part' is fully important as the belief in winning. 'Taking part' means trying to win, and trying to win is as vital to sport as winning. Maybe more so. Winning is what you want to do, and what you try your absolute best to do—because if you don't try, if you don't really take part, you cheat yourself and you cheat your opponent and you cheat your sport."[LIV]

the ones most likely to be spun for a positive. This is damning for a sporting theory based on zero-sum. Consider what Nuke has to say about his lowest point in pickleball:

> *"I was playing with a lower-level player, lower than me, and I think I was just in a crappy mood. I told her, 'You've gotta take that shot!' [said with bite] Which is unlike me to ever talk like that, to anybody . . . And right in that moment, I was like, what the hell is wrong with you? It made me aware to never do that again. I made her feel bad! I'm not trying to make anybody feel bad. So, I'm glad it happened because I know I made her feel bad, and I apologized to her afterward. I'm like, 'Man, I'm so sorry.' But I'm glad it happened because it'll never happen again. And it never has happened again."*

Consider also Thor's lowest point. Going into a professional tournament determined to break a subpar pattern of performance, Thor lost an hour-long first-round waltz and then found no time to rest due to being sucked in as a warm-up partner for multiple acquaintances. Because of this, he won his next match but lost the one after, "playing awful," which caused him to be so pissed off he even cried a little bit. And yet, he says:

> *"It was [a success] . . . Not in the sense that I got my name out there more and improved my ranking, but in the sense that I learned that when it's singles day, I just need to focus on myself. Get myself ready. The top guys in the tournament, like Ben Johns, I never see that guy unless he's on court. He disappears. I don't know where he goes. A lot of the top guys do that. I learned that I just need to focus on myself, get myself prepared, and do my own thing. Don't be talking to other people. I think socializing to a certain extent is fine, but I'm there to play pickleball."*

In both cases, Nuke and Thor experienced a serious failure yet became better off because of it. Ultimately, then, were their experiences not successes? Would it have been preferable for them to have had a more positive moment but then not to have learned an important lesson? In the least, the fact that players are able to find positives in negative experiences makes any zero-sum, plus-minus accounting of wins and losses rather unhelpful.

All in all, it seems that the terms "winning" and "losing," at a minimum, are as equally subjective as they are objective. What it means to win and to lose is, to a large extent, socially constructed and experienced very differently from individual to individual and from situation to situation. There is no straight line that can be drawn from winning to success and from losing to failure. There can very well be a situation in which both sides succeed (i.e., both sides "win") or in which both sides come away from the experience more enriched than when they started. Indeed, it seems that these are the majority of outcomes that occur, at least in pickleball and likely in other sports, too.

11

APP DAYTONA BEACH OPEN

IN THE SECOND WEEK OF FEBRUARY and the third week of the Spring semester, the biggest pickleball tournament of my career is upon me. I am entered in pro singles and pro doubles at the APP Daytona Beach Open and will be spending half of my monthly graduate assistant salary to make it happen. I run sprints on the treadmill for two days in a desperate attempt to get my fitness ready, though it's unlikely to matter much. I am only able to play once in the week leading up to the tournament; Py, Py's son, and The Professor meet me at a middle school gym and work hard to give me a satisfying practice, for which I am grateful. They rotate between themselves to challenge me in skinny singles and then two-versus-one. I also break out a new paddle given to me by Juke, the Selkirk 002. I will use it only this once before traveling to the tournament.

I fly into Orlando late Tuesday night and am met at the airport by Papa Rosey, the father of my doubles partner, along with Papa Rosey's good friend and his good friend's son. We make the hour-long journey to Papa Rosey's friend's house just outside of Daytona Beach, where I will be graciously hosted for the rest of the week. I claim a couch as my own, then go on a midnight jaunt to Denny's to get a sweat going and knock the jet lag. The air is pleasant but thicker than I'm used to and slightly out of my comfort zone. I use the time to run my mind through what is mentally, physically, and emotionally needed to be fully prepared for singles on Thursday. More than simply wanting a good showing, I feel like I don't have much choice. There's a lot on the line: money, pride, research, and the halo of expectations that surrounds a big fish from a small pond. I am also aware that Trayvon Martin was killed mere miles away in a similar setting through which I am now roaming free and unbothered, so this is on my mind, too.

I wake up at 6:00 AM the next morning on five hours of sleep and travel with Papa Rosey to the first day of the tournament. APP (and PPA) tournaments feature and promote the pros, but hundreds of players of all ages and levels compete alongside them in amateur draws, contributing to a vibrant yet chaotic atmosphere. Players stream into the registration office, creating a hive-like buzzing as Papa Rosey checks in for his matches in the age 60+ doubles division. The buzzing is part nervous energy, part giddy excitement and emanates from adults who suddenly get to be like children again. We walk to Papa Rosey's assigned court and meet up with his partner, an easy-going yet competitive fellow from Michigan who linked up with Papa Rosey through the "Players Needing Partners" feature.[1] I spend some time warming them up until the arrival of their opponents and then make a quick perusal of the grounds.

The tournament site, called Pictona, is home to an astounding fifty permanent pickleball courts, all of which are filled at various points during events. The main hubs of activity are a building in the front and a large undercover area turned into a grandstand in the back. Between them lie booths of vendors of various pickleball merchandise and other relevant services of interest, in addition to a deli. Courts sprawl in every corner and orbit the grandstand. The grandstand itself features high school baseball-style bleachers around a central court, with VIP seating directly encircling the court and two hospitality tents for players near the outside ring. Also of note is a makeshift podium for medalists and, of course, the inescapable and interminable **pop** sound of pickleballs on paddles.

Back with Papa Rosey and Co., I try to fulfill my ad hoc duties as coach, emotional support staff, and photographer. The pairing gets slightly outclassed in the first round, rebounds for a win in the back draw, and then ends the day with a comeback effort that comes up just short in the second back

---

1. Each of them arrived several days in advance, so they had the opportunity to practice with each other twice before the tournament. That said, they were essentially strangers, which is neither unusual nor particularly awkward for pickleball, considering how smoothly one can integrate into unfamiliar groups. Frequently, I have observed the "small world" phenomenon, where new pickleball acquaintances make seemingly improbable third-party connections, as was the case here. The two of them came to the realization that Papa Rosey's partner had recently supplied a crematorium to one of Papa Rosey's closest friends.

draw match. Papa Rosey's spirits are down, as he failed to meet the 2-2 goal he'd set for himself and the team and feels they "should have gotten the last one." He quickly turns into the ultimate manager, however, and vows to aid me with anything and everything that I need for the rest of the week.

At the moment, my biggest need is practice, so he and I claim space on a satellite court of the grandstand that is not being used for matches. Despite our sizable gap in ability, Papa Rosey tries his hardest to provide me with resistance in a number of creatively structured drills.[2] In true pickleball fashion, however, we are interrupted by several different teams hoping to share the court to warm up for their matches. We end up playing extensive practice points against two men's and two women's teams ranging from ages 50-60+ and 4.0-5.0 level, making several new friends in the process. As we leave to spend the rest of the day at New Smyrna Beach, I take comfort in the fact that although it may not have been the best tune-up for my game, it was at least productive for others.

I wake up the next morning at 5:00 AM and take a twenty-minute shower. I managed to sleep for only five hours again, this time on and off due to the gallon of Pedialyte-infused water I drank the night before for hydration. My body is awake and alert, however, as the anticipation of playing is already coursing through me. The warm water soothes my nerves while I do little boxing motions and run through a mental checklist of

---

2. Turns out, Papa Rosey may have overdone it. A few hours later, he complained of hip pain, which showed no interest in waning throughout the week. No treatments helped, including those of the psychoactive variety. Then, a little over a month later . . . *voila!* Papa Rosey was equipped with a new artificial hip. Pickleball may feel less than strenuous at times, but it's tougher on the body than it seems, and the risk for injury is ever present.

all I need to remember to be successful. *On drives, aim for the tape. After the return, light split step and go. Expect to be down so that you're prepared for it when it happens.* The words of Andre Agassi faintly echo in the back of my mind, that many of his matches were "won in the afternoon shower,"[LV] and I do my best to maximize this time to fully orient myself to the upcoming drama that is about to take place.

Due to being placed in the qualifying draw, I arrive at Pictona with Papa Rosey at 7:00 AM to warm up. For some reason, I have a slight aversion to formal racquet bags, or just "looking good" in general,[3] so I come equipped with a large Publix paper bag[4] full of mandarins, a loaf of bread, a banana, three Quest power bars, two RX power bars, and fourteen Pedialyte powders to go along with a gallon jug of water.

I make my way to one of the few open courts, jog, and hit a few balls with a supremely stiff Papa Rosey, then replace him with a newly acquainted fellow who also hopes to qualify. The two of us get along well and complete a full warm-up; we even play a rally-scoring[5] match to twenty-one and then a shorter one to seven. I win, but I play terrible. I miss an alarming number of returns that float long, and I begin to wonder if

---

3. For the longest time, I carried my paddles in the manufacturer's plastic package from the very first pickleball paddle I ever owned. I have now moved on to a newer, roomier manufacturer's package, and regrettably, I may be forced to use a real bag soon.

4. Almost exactly one year later, I came back to Florida and again used a Publix paper bag to earn my second APP medal, this time in doubles with Erik Lange. I'm beginning to think grocery bags are my good luck charm.

5. Rally scoring means every point won by a side is a point won, regardless of who is serving. This is different from traditional pickleball, in which one must be serving to be awarded a point.

I'm not dreadfully under-practiced and/or under-accustomed to the new paddle.

Although I am generally confident in myself and expect to qualify, I am fully aware that it could all be over in minutes. Partly, this is because I have a history of slow starts, and partly, this is because rally-scoring to twenty-one is used for the qualifying, which greatly adds to the element of randomness. Players must also win three matches to qualify so that only four out of thirty-two players will advance. Pickleball is young enough that many "ringers," or unknown yet highly skilled players, litter the qualifying draws, and the competition for the few qualifying spots is fierce. Indeed, I am a ringer, but I could also be a ringer who is quickly sent home by another ringer.

My first opponent, fortunately, decides not to show up. This is fortunate mostly from a fitness perspective, though my adrenaline level drops, and it ensures that my first opponent will already have some rhythm while I will not. I look over to the court with my potential opponents and notice seasoned tennis strokes and a skilled game. My soon-to-be first opponent, Collin Shick, is still in his sweatpants and toying with the other player with the languid look that can only come over someone who is not being challenged. I am on alert and prepare for a worthy contest.

It is around this time that Papa Rosey's brother, Rocky, shows up. Rocky is a character straight out of my favorite movie, *The Big Lebowski*, with a quick and zany wit that has the potential to make utterances that have never been heard before by humanity. He and Papa Rosey form my core team and share the honor of carrying my grocery bag. They also act as my sponsors, physical therapists, pep talkers, and court jesters. They seem to genuinely enjoy the spirit of the event, and I feel blessed to have them in my corner.

Not soon after, Shick and I find ourselves on the court. We make small talk and connect over the college tennis experience, in which I learn that he is a recent graduate of North Carolina State. I like him, which puts me at ease somewhat. I also notice that he takes off his sweatpants, a clear sign that he respects me as a player and is taking things seriously. Despite my worries of a slow start, I jump out to a 10-4 lead, which stretches to 11-5 when we switch sides. My hold on the match starts to slip, however, as the other side faces the sun and an annoying glare inhibits my movement and assertiveness just enough to be significant. He chips away at my lead until it's 19-15, then rips a forehand that clips the net and wildly redirects for a winner. I start to feel the pressure, but my general disposition to these frustrating "let court" instances is one of mild amusement at the chaos that's built into the universe. Let courts also tend to even out in the long run.

Sure enough, at 19-17, I hit a stretch volley that hits the top of the net and dribbles over, giving him no chance to return the ball and giving me three match points. I then close out the match 21-18 to survive and advance. As we shake hands, I tell him it's unfortunate that we had to play so early since we both deserve to qualify.[6]

---

6. Later in the day, I told my team that Shick was better than the majority of players that I played in the main draw. Sure enough, just weeks later, Shick qualified for a PPA draw and tore through the bottom half to reach the finals. Shick then took the first game off the number one player, Ben Johns, before falling in three games to take silver—mirroring and effectively bettering what I did in Daytona (from a results perspective). I have to imagine the experience of our match had some effect on his subsequent success.

Though I'm happy for the victory, it's obvious that Lady Fortuna could have just as easily smiled in a different direction. I also have very little time to feel good (or bad) about myself, as my final qualifying match is called within minutes. I'm matched up with a tall, baby-faced sixteen-year-old named Jayden Broderick, whom I had casually chatted with before. He's a nice kid with skilled shots, but the gap in age and high-level competitive experience gives me a huge edge. The match goes in my favor without too much tension, 21-10, though I feel that he could be a force in due time.

Now that I've qualified for the main draw, I have a little over an hour to rest and get ready. Papa Rosey, Rocky, and I go into the grandstand area and claim a corner of the bleachers, which then becomes our base camp for the rest of the tournament. Conveniently located in the front row and facing Center Court, it is easy for us to rest, view matches, and socialize with people passing by. As would become a pattern, I slam food from my Publix bag and chug enough Pedialyte water to provide homes for several goldfish. In particular, the heavily diluted, unappetizing taste of Pedialyte water becomes very comforting, like a lifeline on a quiz show or a notecard on an open-book test. I sense that it will have a direct impact on the story that is written for the day, as will the rest of my provisions.

For my first main-draw match, I draw the number four seed, Ryler DeHeart, as the "lowly" qualifiers are matched up against the highest-seeded players. DeHeart is an ex-professional tennis player who advanced to the second round of the 2008 US Open (where he fell to Rafael Nadal), and I respect his game. We are also familiar with each other on the pickleball court since we squared off in the back draw of my first professional

event in Alabama months earlier. On that occasion, I was fortunate to come away a winner, and the match ended with an
impressive slinging of the paddle across the court, over the
fence, and into a thicket of trees just outside the arena. To
warm up, I enlist the help of an understandably glum-looking
Collin Shick, who is courteous enough to aid his ex-opponent.
I make a pledge to root for him in the future.

DeHeart and I are placed on a peripheral court around
10:45 AM. There is a slight breeze, and the Florida sun reaches
its high point for the day, shining down at mid-eighties
Fahrenheit. The vibes are different from our last encounter, as
there seems to be a strong sense of mutual respect. We attract
a small crowd, with a contingent of DeHeart's friends and
family on one side, Papa Rosey and Rocky on the other, and
an additional smattering of mostly neutral observers, including
friends John Cincola and M1. I come out like gangbusters and
cruise to an 11-2 victory in the first game, though DeHeart
does not play his best. Midway through the game, an interesting moment occurs in which the referee gives my team a formal
warning for coaching after one of them whispers something to
me like "Let's go" or "Keep it up" between points. We protest
that they're just generally supporting, but I raise my arms in
slight exasperation and say, "My fault, it's not a big deal,"
when the back-and-forth gets to be argumentative.[7] I actively
try to project playful kindness to referees in recognition of their
difficult position, which usually garners me some sympathy,
but this ref is ultra-serious and is having none of it.

---

7. This incident then became a repeated topic of conversation among my team
for the rest of the week. Rocky even approached the ref later for a conversation,
memorably stating, "Ma'am, I am not even capable of coaching him."

After we switch sides for the second game, I remind myself that DeHeart is sure to play better and go on a run, so I must stay strong. It is easier to say than do, however, and I quickly get into a sizable hole. Now that I'm facing the sun, I also begin to get wildly out of breath. I attribute this to mild heat stroke—a serious problem I used to have on first contact with heat and humidity as a Seattle-based tennis player. This is very disconcerting, and I come to the realization that my fitness level is just not where it needs to be to give my best effort in this match and in the tournament more generally. I lose the second game as badly as I won the first, 11-2.

For the third game, I get a bit of a second wind, and though physically I'm less than fresh, the competition is thoroughly enjoyable. Our efforts are well-matched, and the overall product is much more successful. After an epically long point, I call timeout and pant against the side fence while, good-naturedly, DeHeart quips, "Oh good, then I'll use my timeouts later," insinuating he, too, is feeling the hurt. He goes to the corner and converses playfully with his two adorable little kids, who give him earnest tips on how to keep going. This makes me smile. The match then continues in cordial yet fierce competition. I am actually overruled on a ball that I thought was close but out, and DeHeart seems to accept my apology. The tipping point comes at 8-9, when I am in control of a long point while at the net, but then hit a backhand several feet long on an easy ball that my body just gives out on. DeHeart then closes out the game and the match, 11-8, letting out a guttural "*Come on!*" with a complementary hunched-over fist pump.

Our team regroups on the bleachers in palpable disappointment, though I am too tired to feel too unhappy. Mainly,

I berate myself for not being in better shape. My spirits are lifted when Rocky unexpectedly appears with a newly purchased purple APP shirt to replace my now marshy purple University of Washington shirt. I am touched by this act of kindness and immediately make the switch, which feels *great*. Even with this, though, my physical and emotional morale is medium-low as I trudge out for my first back draw match versus a friendly chap named Austin O'Reilly.

By this point, I completely forgo warm-up, mostly in an effort to conserve energy but also partially because of a subconscious fatalism that has crept into the back of my mind. I prepare for the journey to end basically at any moment, though for this match, it becomes apparent that my opponent and I are on different levels. I hit decent shots but never feel fully present and move around almost casually. O'Reilly is a fine player—indeed, he would go on to win the 5.0 35+ bracket—but my mind wanders to Shick and other failed qualifiers that would have been more deserving of an automatic bid. I win 15-2. O'Reilly seems disgusted with his performance and hurries off the court. I feel a little melancholy and wish for his sake that he felt better about his performance.

In my next match, I draw a short and burly fellow from Mexico, Frank Solana, who also had to qualify and who already defeated a skilled friend of mine. My mind is effectively blank, with all expectations having flown the coop. I would not be surprised if I start to cramp. We chat briefly in Spanish before starting our dance. Interestingly, this is the match I would recall the least later, but also the only match that I would have the pleasure of reviewing, as somebody would post a recording of it on YouTube. Solana is a feisty player who really makes the rallies extend, and we are neck and neck early. He takes a modest lead, then makes an egregious call on a perfect backhand down-the-line passing shot of mine with a clear line of sight for the both of us. I immediately protest, though not to the referee, who is standing on the opposite side and thus unlikely to overrule. Solana claims it missed by an "inch," but I call bull. I turn around and whisper to myself, "Fuck this guy."[8]

From this point forward, my emotional intensity spikes to a level that raises my play, and I hit some dazzling shots, including an ATP on the dead run and a bending down-the-line forehand pass which elicits a sharp reaction from the small crowd. I move on to the next round with a 15-7 victory.

At about this time, the remaining players are given a brief lunch break, for which I am grateful. I eat an APP-provided veggie wrap and yogurt and feel a mini burst of energy. Rocky also starts to vigorously roll out my legs with a muscle stick of unknown provenance. I should probably roll out my muscles more often, but either because I'm lazy or just genetically lucky, I'm not used to it, and it makes me squirm like a rambunctious puppy who's been held too long. The sensation is a cross between a pressing pain and the feeling of blood rushing back into a body part that has fallen asleep, especially when approaching the hip flexor. All in all, I feel marginally refreshed and ready to put forth a decent effort in the next match.

By the time I am on court for match number seven (counting the warm-up match), approximately seven hours have passed and the sun has disappeared, leaving behind a formidable gust in

---

8. This is meant as an honest depiction of what I was thinking and feeling at the time, not as an attack on Solana's character. In fact, Solana gave me a hearty congratulations at the medal ceremony, and there were no issues outside of this moment.

the direction parallel to the court. My opponent, Eden Lica, is a towering ex-tennis player from Romania with a goofy personality to whom I promptly take a liking. He has the best haircut in the tournament: a mohawk that reminds me of the cover art of Audioslave's album *Cochise*. As we begin play, I feel the score should be modified to reflect the three—not two—competitors on the court: Eden, me, and the *wind*, which proceeds to comically alter how some points are played. I start with my shots going with the wind, which is not my preferred position in pickleball due to how difficult it is to keep the ball down on such a short court. Into the wind, I feel like I can swing to high heaven since the ball slows down so much. Lica, on the other hand, prefers the opposite, so when we switch sides, and I hit a backhand return that is pushed back at me by Mother Nature, humorously, he says, "Yes, now *I* have the good side!" To my benefit, however, I manage to create a sizable lead, then get stuck on fourteen before closing it out, 15-10.

Back at home base, team morale has risen greatly since the defeat to DeHeart, but physically, the tank is almost empty. I am dead tired, and it feels like I can't go on much longer. I express this to my team, but they want to hear none of it. Papa Rosey was a collegiate wrestler and Olympic alternate in Greco-Roman, and "can't" is not really in his vocabulary. He tells me a personal story about a pep talk given to him by the legendary wrestler and wrestling coach Dan Gable, with the basic message being, "Oh, you think you're *tired?*" I have no intention of folding my hand, but my doubts are sincere, and to have a sounding board like this is invaluable. I continue to shove food and water in my mouth and await my possible execution.

I prefer not to look at draws and know who I am to play next. I have found that this largely causes me to develop preconceived notions about what can, should, or will happen, in addition to judgments of my opponent's skill vis-a-vis mine, none of which is helpful. Thus, even though I am a bit in doom and gloom mode, when I am told my next opponent is William Sobek, I begin to acquire a false sense of security.

Sobek is a good player and very experienced, but in singles, I imagine myself to be in a half-class above. One look at his backhand, and I can tell he's never played tennis, nor has anyone formally taught him the stroke as he comes across the ball with a sort of sidespin. As a snobbish tennis player, this gives me confidence. Sobek is also barely old enough to vote and is under immense pressure from his team. On the other hand, he competes hard and plays very fair despite the pressure, which I deeply respect. Considering my physical state, I am nervous that I may take a loss that I will not be happy with.

I get down 4-0 in what feels like thirty seconds. *Oh, here we go*, I think, and call a timeout. I rebuke myself for the silly thoughts earlier—this kid's good! What's more, I may be in serious trouble as my tank may truly be empty. I manage to push these thoughts away, however, and adopt a new mentality: *just one more step, one more shot, one more point*. Everything is reduced to the bare minimum. I have no emotions; good or bad shot, win or lose the point, it's the same. No wasted energy. Between points, I walk at a languid pace and go to my towel on the fence. The to-and-fro and the touch of the fibers on my face become comforting and ritualistic.

Somehow, with this new rhythm, I climb back to near-even at the halfway switch, then take the lead. At one point, I try an ill-advised topspin lob, and Sobek shanks it thirty feet over the fence. I hear Sobek's coach let out a loud groan, and I turn to my team near the back fence and whisper, "Thank *God.*" I call timeout again just to breathe, then stretch the lead to 14-9 before he calls timeout. At nearly every timeout, I hear Sobek bickering with his team, and at this moment, his coach accuses him of quitting. I feel like the match is over, but Sobek comes out properly motivated and fights like an animal pushed to the edge of a cliff. Finally, the ball bounces my way. I close it out, 15-12.

Relieved to win, the team goes through the usual rigama-role at home base, and then I am back in the torture chamber before long. A longer break would be nice, but I feel like I'd need a full week to be fresh.[9] My next opponent, I'm happy to learn, is Marshall Brown, my choice for friendliest player on the men's Pro Tour.[10] I'm pleased that if someone is going to put me out of my misery, it will be Marshall. Alternatively, Marshall and I have actually played already in Alabama, and I gave him a pretty decisive beat down. It would be at least a little disappointing to lose to a player who struggled to score any points against me the time before.

Similar to our Alabama match, and despite my physical condition, I rage out to a 9-2 lead. Marshall is a solid player, so I'm not sure why I see his ball so well. Then, suddenly, my energy level starts reaching critical levels—fast—and I am in

---

9. This would turn out to be all too true. I have never felt such soreness in my life. Two days later, in doubles, my body seized up if I stopped activity for more than five minutes, and it took at least a week to feel normal again.

10. There are so many class acts in pickleball, but honorable mentions of friendliest men's players that I have experience with include Stefan Auvergne, Augie Ge, James Chaudry, Phillip Locklear, Ben Newell, and Richard Livornese Jr.

free fall. In the past few matches, there were balls that I hobbled to and made a mess of, yet I managed to laugh them off as if my physical deterioration was amusing. Now, there doesn't seem to be anything funny about the situation—it's code red. I experience the lactic acid build-up like weights in my bone marrow, and it reminds me of a college tennis match that I played versus Cal Poly two days after I had serious food poisoning. Every recovery period feels like an hourglass jammed with honey; every move is like trying to trek through snow. Small flickers of muscle spasms suggest cramps on the horizon. Marshall surges back amidst this malaise for an 11-10 lead, and the end times are well in sight.

Feeling no better, I manage to tie the score back up 11-11, and then something wondrous happens. A friend of mine, Nasty, shows up at the fence and bellows out a loud, "LET'S GO PURPLE JESUS!" The deadness in the air surrounding me and my team evaporates immediately, and this act of friendly enthusiasm seems to ripple through me and infuse me with new life. With a smile on my face, I turn to him and give an appreciative chuckle. I consider it like magic. What feels like less than a minute later, I am victorious, 15-11. Marshall, the good sport, is very congratulatory, though I know he must feel some disappointment from what was probably an excellent opportunity to advance.

Staring down the barrel of yet another match, what will be the tenth, my mind is whizzing with thoughts of mind over matter. I am learning about myself, what I'm capable of, and what artificial impediments I create to get in my own way. There seems to be a reserve of energies within me that I didn't know was there. Even so, I still believe that I have virtually no chance in the next match, which is against none other than my old friend Ryler DeHeart. The double-elimination format of pickleball makes these unique rematches possible, though thus far, our paths to the rematch have been dissimilar, to say the least. DeHeart has played a whopping six fewer matches than I have. My only goal is to play one point at a time and come out standing.

I cross paths with DeHeart before the match and he says to me, "I can't believe I'm seeing you again. You're a warrior." You and me both, pal. And thank you.

To my surprise, my body never feels quite as torn down as it did versus Marshall, and I grab an early lead and never look back. I climb all the way to 14-7 and take my second timeout, reasoning that I should be able to nab the last point while semi-rested. For that matter, I have used my timeouts brilliantly all day, either by opportunely securing rest or by interrupting my opponent's momentum.

However, just like Sobek, the last point proves to be elusive. DeHeart is a world-class competitor, of course, so I expect nothing less. Then, improbably, Nasty once again makes an impact on my match. Nasty and DeHeart have a rather infamous history together, which may explain why, after Nasty throws a couple of cheers my way, DeHeart rather shockingly yells from the other side of the court, "Oh hey, it's my favorite person! Why don't you cheer for *me*, [Nasty]?" Moments after this break in concentration, I finally score the final point to win, 15-9. I then walk off in some degree of disbelief.

After the match, someone tells me I am in the money since I am now guaranteed fourth place. The payout for fourth is $375 with a full reimbursement of all fees for a total value of $745. It astounds me that this did not cross my mind *once* while playing. To some degree, I still find it a bit surreal that I'm all the way in Daytona Beach in a pickleball tournament, let alone for money. Here I am in my thirties, playing a backyard game, creating, and, in some sense, *reliving* high-level athletic memories. When I quit tennis and moved to Indonesia to teach English, I figured my athletic heights and highlights were behind me. Maybe that wasn't true and there's still more to come.

In addition, though my mind and body are mostly numb at this point, I do sense something that could be metaphysical, and most certainly beautiful. Slowly, throughout the day, I have managed to accumulate support from a number of unexpected and often unfamiliar corners. This includes peeps from my home state (some old friends, some new), players Papa Rosey and I warmed up the day before, players in qualifying, opponents, family of opponents, observers of unknown relation (with whom subtle connections were made), and a very warm and enthusiastic older couple[11]—all in addition to Papa Rosey, Rocky, and the close friends I already knew would be there. I begin to feel like I am somehow absorbing the wills, hopes, energies, and positive vibes from all these people, which surround me like "spren" in Brandon Sanderson's *The Stormlight Archive*. I am myself, of course, but maybe for this brief, divine period, I am also more than myself, like a Frankenstein of foreign parts given freely and powerfully out of love.

---

11. My relationship with this couple has since grown, and I now am proud to say that I have a "pickleball mother."

My support system reaches a crescendo in the match prior to the bronze medal match,[12] as it seems virtually everyone in the decently-sized crowd is on my side, or at least not against me. My opponent is Andrei Daescu, a very tall, hyper-focused player from Romania who is elite in doubles. I no longer doubt myself, mostly because I no longer know what is appropriate to expect from myself. I am in a mode of total surrender to the whims of chance and the unknown—a "let's just see what happens" attitude, so to speak. The match starts, and the play is pretty equal. Daescu is excellent at the "cat-and-mouse" strategy, almost playing singles like it's doubles by dropping balls in the kitchen and coming forward. His reach is so long it's hard to get the ball by him, even if it feels like I'm in a good position. He takes a small lead. Then, near the midway point, I hit a lightly floating backhand return that hits the inside part of the sideline, and Daescu calls it out.

Now, through more than twenty years of trials and tribulations in tennis, I have learned that there's a distinct difference between a missed call and what tennis players call a "hook." Everyone misses calls; we're human, and we don't have Hawk-Eye technology in our retina.[13] A hook is more of a deliberately

---

12. In this case, the "bronze medal match" is the match in which the loser takes third place (bronze) and the winner advances to possibly win gold. In other cases, where there is no double-elimination wrap-around, the winner simply takes third place.

13. As a note for the uninitiated, in tennis and in pickleball, players must call the balls that land on their side, i.e., the ones *hit by their opponents*, in or out. If a ball is in and can be retrieved, nothing is actually called, and play simply continues. If it is in and not retrieved, players usually say "good" or "in" or make a gesture of a flat hand with the palm facing downward, or they may do nothing. If a ball is out, players must make a verbal call (usually "out" or "long" or "wide") or a hand gesture (usually a raised index finger like "number one"). Since players call their

missed call (i.e., cheating), and in this case, I feel I am being hooked. Considering the money that's on the line, it's understandable to *want* the ball to be out, and it's also possible that it's more negligent than deliberate, but it still leaves a sour taste in my mouth.

Interestingly, the call occurs on the same court, the same line, and near the same spot as the instance with Solana many moons ago, but unlike that time, this ball is floating and thus easier to see. I protest, not to the referee, who declines to overrule, but to my opponent, who naturally gets defensive and claims, "You weren't even on the line!" This gets me fired up because we basically had similar vantage points, not exactly on the line but well near it. I know I will not change his mind, but in this instant, I leave my mode of surrender to the universe and burn with an objective arising straight from Freud's Id: I want to *win*. Moments later, I hit a great shot and make a big fist pump in the air, arguably in Daescu's direction. The gesture feels alien, like it didn't really come from me, and makes me feel a little icky, though mostly in hindsight.

We switch sides, with Daescu leading 8-5. On one of the first points after the switch, I approach the net after a return and get a paddle on a first volley, which is weak, and Daescu rips a forehand down the line that I cannot touch. The ball lands very near the baseline, possibly in, but without hesitation, I call it out. The referee, though he is standing closer to this line, again does not overrule, and Daescu (rightfully) flips out. He confronts

---

opponents' balls, the system leans heavily on honesty, so unfortunately, it is quite easy to cheat. If there is a referee, they can assist if they have a definitive look, but this is not always the case. On rare occasions, mostly in pro tournaments, video replay and a player challenge system is used.

me angrily, to which I say, "It was just as far out as my shot," pointing to where my ball had landed. "*Oh*, that's how we're gonna play this, huh?" is his response, and I shoot back with, "Hell yeah, that's how we're playing this. Now we're even."

Play continues, and the next several points are obviously intense. I regret the situation—I am at my most comfortable when cordiality and sportsmanship reign supreme—but I do not regret my action. In my experience, a tit-for-tat strategy is the only thing that solves the issue or sets things straight, assuming it is very clear what happened in the first place and assuming the other player knows very clearly what the tit-for-tat action means.[14]

A few points later, Daescu hits another ball in a similar area to the most recent controversial call, but this time, the ball is well out by about two inches. I call it out, and Daescu scolds the ref for not overruling, even using the ref's first name, saying, "If you're too tired, [ref's name], we can get somebody else!" I find this to be overly personal and mean-spirited, but obviously, Daescu is still hot. Overall, I think he respects my tit-for-tat in a *mano-a-mano* competitive sort of way. Whether I am right about any of this—i.e., the "hook," my decision, my perception of my opponent's behavior, etc.—the rest of the match does unfold without issue and is, in fact, supremely fair. I consciously try to play any ball near the line to hold up my end of the implicit bargain. When tides start to turn my way and Daescu calls a timeout, I go up to him on the sideline

---

14. There is very strong evidence that this might actually be true, presented by Robert Axelrod in *The Evolution of Cooperation*. When there is a defection, the strategy that is most often the best, in the long-term, is for the second player to immediately defect as well, i.e., a "tit-for-tat" strategy.

and offer to tap paddles, a sign of respect which, thankfully, he reciprocates.

Like so many previous matches, the last point is the toughest to get. At 14-10, the victory is just within reach, yet I can't quite realize it, with three, four, five tries, like a sporting version of Tantalus in a pool of water. At each failure, I walk to my towel on the back fence, keep my cool, and mutter to a guy with dreads who happens to be standing there. He starts to mutter back simple words of encouragement, and we develop a momentary bond. Finally, at 14-13, with Daescu knocking on the doorstep, I sink my teeth into a booming forehand passing shot that lands well in. I let out a spastic celebratory grunt that comes deep from within.

Endorphins flood in. The crowd claps as we shake hands, though Daescu has some choice words for the referee and a few audience members before exiting the scene in a hurry.

Making my exit, I thank all of those who supported me and accept numerous congratulatory gestures en route back to home base. I am now due for $625, or $995 total, which this time *was* somewhat on my mind since it completely pays for my expenses and even gives me some pocket money. It certainly feels earned, as I am fully numb to my body and, to some extent, to reality. It is clear that I have undergone a highly liminal experience; I am no longer who I was before the tournament started, neither as a player nor as a person. I, or more accurately, we, have *done* this.

Nevertheless, there is still more to do, insanely. I am now set up to play my twelfth match of the day versus one of the Johnson twins for a chance to compete in the finals on Championship Sunday, which will be shown on ESPN2.

I spend some time watching their intensely competitive match, which ends with Yates defeating his brother and the number-one seed, Hunter, in a mild upset. Hunter, it is, then. More than anything, I'm just relieved it will all be over soon.

Because our match will be a featured match, we must wait for the women's round to finish and Center Court to open. During this time, Rocky graciously purchases another veggie wrap from the deli for me. By now, I have eaten almost everything in my grocery bag, save some power bars, and have drunk over five gallons of Pedialyte water. A new friend and fellow player also tries to give me pointers on what to expect from Hunter Johnson and how to play, which I appreciate, though quietly, I marvel at how any person in their right mind thinks I might now be able to take down the best player in the tournament, two out of three games to eleven. All in all, I am afforded about a seventy-five-minute break, which, though taken with pleasure, in hindsight, allows my body to leave its shell-shocked state and stiffen up, likely dooming any sliver of a chance I had.

Dusk creeps in by the time Hunter and I are on Center Court. From the first touch of my sole, a different feeling sets in, produced probably by several cues declaring, "This is it. This is the big time." The artificial lights are much brighter, the court is much more spacious, the camera people are much more focused, and the audience is much more expectant of a good show. There is even a snazzy scoreboard. Doubts sneak in again, as I don't know if I'll be able to physically match others' hopes and expectations for me, let alone win. I tell Hunter, "I'll try my best" to give him a good match, which is more honest than in jest.

Sure enough, an inauspicious omen occurs on the first point when I return Hunter's serve, dart to the net like a tiger, then somehow lose my balance and tumble forward into a piteous heap, drawing blood in three places. Things do not improve much from there. Hunter hits laser-like groundstrokes with sublime precision, and my neck gets well-practiced at twisting backward to see shots land inside the court. I am also impressed with his depth of serve. To my credit, though, the match is not completely devoid of drama. Midway through the first game, we play a long point that stretches me wide to the backhand, for which I sell out and roast an ATP. Hunter scrambles to it and just manages to flick it off the ground for a slow floating winner that seems to playfully mock me on its way down. The crowd erupts in applause, and all I can do is cheer along.

From this point forward, it may be fair to say that my body and mind understandably join forces to throw in the towel, not in effort, per se, but in competition. Hunter is already a little better than me, or at least better trained, and short of a life-and-death-provoking scenario like that of Ernest Shackleton on the *Endurance*, to expect anything more from my body may not be realistic. Even when Nasty yells out, "Purple Jesus RISES!" the magic seems to have left the building.

Contrarily, it may be fair to say that I finally commit the competitor's cardinal sin and give up, as I use *none* of my timeouts, which my team will later point to as a disappointment. I am reminded of a time back in college tennis, when, after upsetting the NCAA's sixty-third-ranked player in the quarterfinals of a regional tournament—down 5-2 in each of the second and third sets and facing multiple match points over three and a half hours of play—I then played the semifinals versus a top-thirty player on the same day. Though I competed well in the first set, I had nothing left in the second set and lost 6-0. Afterward, I remember overhearing our head coach talking quite positively about my effort to our assistant coach, yet with a little nugget at the end of their conversation that will stick with me forever: ". . . but, he *still* went soft there at the end." Is it possible that at the end of this potentially transcendental experience, after playing the most matches the format allows, I went *soft*? Did I actually have more to give? Am I hearing the "*tsk tsk*" of ghosts of my better selves?

Hunter wins the match 11-5, 11-1, and gives me a friendly "great run" when we shake hands. I clap my paddle in the air in an affectionate gesture to the crowd, noticing that several of my supporters are still around. I glance at the clock on the scoreboard and see something poetic: stepping on the court for warm-up at 7:15 AM, I now step off the court for the final time at 7:15 PM, twelve hours later.

Swiftly, I change out of my now fetid purple APP shirt, which I had kept on for eight matches out of superstition. Papa Rosey, Rocky, and I then finally start the journey home and later celebrate with beers and grub at a restaurant that features gator meat. I find the idea of this enjoyable, even as a vegetarian. Sitting back in my chair, I think, "What is not to enjoy in this life after a day like today?"

Recap of the Day's Events

Wake Up	5:00 AM
Arrive at Pictona	7:00 AM
Warm-Up	7:15 AM
Match #1: Default	8:00 AM
Match #2: Collin Shick	8:25 AM
Match #3: Jayden Broderick	8:55 AM
Match #4: Ryler DeHeart	10:30 AM
Match #5: Austin O'Reilly	11:45 AM
Match #6: Frank Solana	12:30 PM
Match #7: Eden Lica	1:45 PM
Match #8: William Sobek	2:40 PM
Match #9: Marshall Brown	3:30 PM
Match #10: Ryler DeHeart	4:15 PM
Match #11: Andrei Daescu	5:00 PM
Match #12: Hunter Johnson	6:45 PM
Leave Pictona	7:30 PM

Agential Realism

If ideas were said to have kin, a close cousin or elder relative of coopetition would be agential realism. In the following chapter, I will lightly use the lens of agential realism to make sense of my experience at APP Daytona Beach. It is not necessary to understand agential realism to enjoy the chapter, but some basics might help. Consider this "Agential Realism for Dummies."

Agential realism is a theory proposed by Karen Barad in the mid-2000s that fuses concepts in quantum physics with the social sciences. Quantum physics is the study of matter at the smallest, most fundamental level, such as electrons and photons (of light). One phenomenon in quantum physics is called "entanglement," which describes how two or more objects (i.e., really tiny particles) are connected in such a way that they act as a *system*, not as independent objects. This means that if something is known about one object, something is also known about the other object(s). As an example, if a pair of entangled objects are known to have zero spin, then finding one object with a clockwise spin indicates that the other object has a counterclockwise spin, *even if they are thousands of miles apart.* If this seems hard to believe, Einstein would agree, as he famously called quantum entanglement "spooky action at a distance" in a letter in 1947. The romantic in me considers this nature's greatest proof that love exists, as if two entangled objects have hearts that beat as one.

Agential realism's core proposal is that all things, human and non-human, are similarly "**entangled**." This means that things exist only as a set of relations with other things. In other words, nothing exists independently or separately from anything else—a twist on the ancient idea that everything is connected. Pronouns like "I" and "you," for instance, set up boundaries between what are actually co-dependents or *co-beings* of the human race, seen perhaps most clearly in the case of mother and child, where the latter exists more in relation to the former than in any independent sense.

With the social and physical world existing in a web of entanglement, agential realism then proposes that things are constantly co-creating each other. This means that instead of *inter*action, which assumes two or more independent things, there is only "**intra-action**," or an *emergence* (i.e., becoming) of things that were already a part of each other in the first place (see Figure 2). An "around the post" (ATP) shot in pickleball, for instance, is not "hit" by one player independently, but instead emerges due to the intra-action of the equipment, the weather, the court, the previous shot hit by the opponent, and the past training, movement, and foresight of the attacking player, among other things.

On this note, intra-action does not need to involve things that are present in time or space. In agential realism, time does not linearly progress in a sequence of past-present-future; instead, space, time, and matter are entangled in what's called "**spacetimemattering**." This means that phenomena are constantly unfolding and woven into one another, like a textile made up of an "infinity of moments-places-matterings,"[LVI] without beginning and without end. The night sky that we see in the "present," for example, sparkles with light from stars in the "past,"[LVII] many of which have since exploded in the time it took for their light to reach Earth, acting as an omen for the "future" of our star, the Sun.

There are many other concepts as well as implications for how reality should be interpreted in agential realism, but I will only quickly mention a few more. First, binaries such as body and mind are more fictional than real. Using "mind-body" might sound funny, yet it may also reflect the intraconnection of reality better. Second, since everything is co-created, ethically, we all share in the blame or praise of an outcome. An individual's failure of performance is partly a collective failure, and an event's rousing success is partly an individual's success. Last, any observation of a situation inevitably makes a "cut" between factors that are included and excluded, despite the inseparability of everything. Many factors go unnoticed, especially if they are not present and obvious, but this does not mean they are less important.

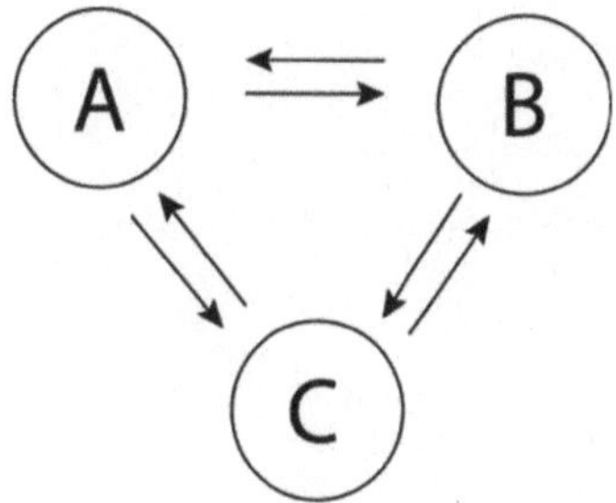

Figure 2 (a). An **interaction**: three independent entities involved in a cause and effect with each other. (Image courtesy of Tess Manthou.)

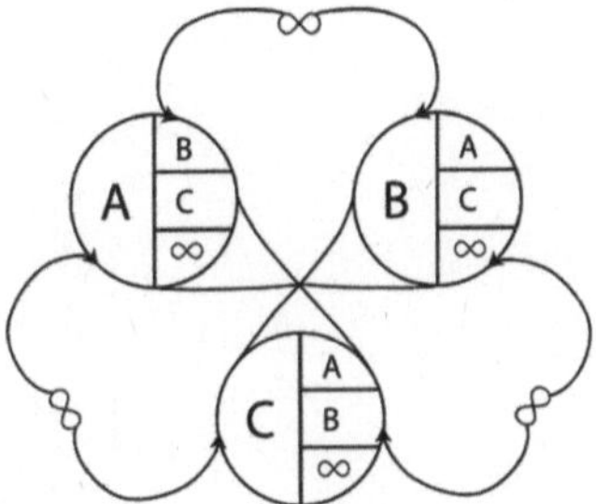

Figure 2 (b). An **intra-action**: three co-dependent entities involved in a *becoming*, with an infinite number of other entities affecting the situation from the background. (Image courtesy of Tess Manthou.)

12

ANALYSIS OF APP DAYTONA BEACH OPEN

MY EXPERIENCE at the APP Daytona Beach Open has become one of the most cherished in my sporting career, not just because of the favorable results but because its lessons run deep. Like any good piece of art, the more I contemplate the experience, the more I take things away from it.

One thing for certain is that the mind-body that makes up my "self" was pushed to perform beyond what I believed to be possible, so much so that I am convinced that "I" can hardly be held responsible.[1]

---

1. It feels like the English language is not equipped to truly describe the experience since I feel compelled, as an English speaker, to use pronouns and possessives like "I" or "my," which feel misleading and inaccurate.

I am simply not capable of doing what I did, as silly as that may sound. My individual effort was minuscule compared to the enormity of intra-actions that allowed for such a performance. The gear, the grub, the supporters, the opponents . . . I would have been nowhere without them, and I am nothing without being in relation to them. It is my hope, dear reader, that what follows will convince you of this fact.

Let us first start with the gear. I did not buy a single article of clothing or equipment used in the competition; they were all gifts. This was not intentional but also not surprising for those who know me well. The hat was gifted to me by my sister, who works for an outdoor apparel company. I have worn it at almost every important competition, partly because it's purple and partly because it reminds me of her.

The boxers, occasionally visible, were gifted to me by my mother, probably at Christmas or for my birthday. I am picky about receiving gifts that I don't need or will not use, so my mother, an enthusiastic gift-giver, has compromised by bi-annually purchasing me boxers with silly designs, which she knows I will wear. It is possible that I was wearing eggplants, mermaids, squirrels with nuts, slabs of butter, or raccoon bandits.

The shoes and socks were gifted to me by Ninja, though at different times in life. Ninja has played the hand-me-down big brother role in my life since I was in elementary school, and recently, I have benefited from his tendency to over-accumulate shoes. There is only so much space in his garage, and I'm sure his wife is thrilled whenever I go home with a souvenir.

The shorts and first shirt were provided by the University of Washington, which were the same ones I wore several years ago as a student-athlete. Our team was given so much gear that I still have apparel with the tags on, waiting to enter my rotation when things wear out. These clothes connect me to my previous self, when I was at my peak athletic performance, and to memories of time shared with some of the most important people in my life.

The second shirt, of course, was bought for me by Rocky, and Juke gifted me with my paddle. Both men have impacted me in memorable ways. Juke, in particular, has been extraordinarily generous and supportive, and the paddle is a conduit for our connection whenever I use it.

I would also be remiss not to mention the likely hundreds of individuals who worked—thanklessly in many cases—to bring the products to my possession. The gear and equipment were manufactured in at least five countries, including Bangladesh, China, Indonesia, Madagascar, and Vietnam. Then, there were those who collected the raw materials, transported the finished materials, or marketed and sold the products. Altogether, I imagine the most diverse neighborhood in London might fail to pass as a microcosm for the diversity of individuals who unknowingly intra-acted to equip me with the proper gear.

In this vein, I give an ode to all those who may have been trapped in modern-day slavery, such as Nasreen Sheikh, and forced to work in sweatshop conditions just so that I could play. I was blessed to hear Nasreen Sheikh speak for Earth Day at Illinois State University at an opportune moment when these thoughts were percolating in my mind. Sheikh says of her time in a sweatshop in Nepal:

"I hated those clothes . . . woven with the energy of my suffering. At the end of each day, I would collapse onto the large bundles of

clothes and daydream about where they would end up and who would wear them. [LVIII]

The energy of suffering may have been woven into my fabrics, in addition to regular toil, the love of my friends and family, and the pride of my university. Beyond the people involved, however, it must finally be said that the *materials* intra-acted as well. I was not simply Purple Jesus, pickleball player; I was Purple Jesus, pickleball player, with a Dri-Fit hat and Dri-Fit shirt to keep my body cool, a set of shoes made for the pickleball surface, soles yet to be overworn (a chronic issue of mine), and a carbon fiber paddle on par with my competitors' paddles.[2] In

A re-creation of the full assembly of gear, including Rocky's shirt. (Image courtesy of the author)

this way, these materials were intra-actors on the way that events transpired, too.

Now, let's consider the grub. An incredible amount of refueling was required to keep my mind-body operating at a sufficient clip. Never in my life had I drunk that much liquid over the course of half a day. The water and electrolytes kept my body hydrated and helped to regulate nerve and muscle function. I also managed

---

2. Technology has changed so quickly in pickleball that many paddles have become obsolete for a high-level tournament player. For instance, the paddle that I used up until one week before Daytona, the Franklin Signature Ben Johns, was actually ridiculed by a random woman while I acted as coach for Papa Rosey. She saw it leaning against a bench and questioned whose it could possibly be, blurting out: "People only use that if they pay them!"

to consume two half-meals and an entire grocery bag of goodies. These nutrients intra-acted with the inner workings of my digestive system so that glucose could be absorbed into the bloodstream and become energy; at the same time, that energy was cycled out onto the court and translated into performance until, finally, the equilibrium could no longer hold. Lucky for me, the maintenance of this virtuous cycle held up basically until the end, though it may have teetered and tottered along the way.

It is also the case that ingesting the amount and kind of nutrients that I did was not an act of great personal wisdom and foresight. My mind-body had been rigorously trained from twenty-plus years of competitive situations. The most potent feedback came from my mother, ever worried about whether I had eaten enough; from my coaches and trainers, particularly those at the University of Washington who demanded that I become more professional; and from trial by fire, when not ingesting enough simply shut me down. The faint echoes of emptiness rattling around in my bones and the stern reproaches from those wanting the best for me were etched into my memory, compelling me to make certain decisions.

Even with this, it took a recent, rocky experience for me to fully prepare to meet the moment. In my first pro tournament a few months earlier, I reached the seventh match of the day and crashed mid-way, unable to bring even a semblance of my normal game. Though very disappointing at the time, this experience paid dividends in Daytona when I more fully appreciated the task at hand and prepared accordingly. Its specter even compelled me to go on a late-night jaunt to Denny's—the only time I paid for a full meal on the trip

A re-creation of all that was consumed over the twelve hours of play
(Image courtesy of the author.)

since most of my eating needs throughout the week were generously covered by Papa Rosey.

Finally, like the gear, it must also be noted that there were hundreds of nameless individuals who worked and toiled to bring the food to market and eventually to my mouth. Their efforts may have been out of sight and mind, yet they were yet were nevertheless required for my performance to have occurred the way it did.

The next category to consider is the supporters, starting with those who made the most tangible effect. Without Papa Rosey and Rocky, I would not have survived much longer than the loss to DeHeart. Both offered very timely contributions that I would not have even thought to request.

Rocky appeared with a fresh shirt just as I started to sag under the sweat of my other shirt, like a crocodile in a swamp. The muscle roller stick also could not have come at a better time and likely kept me from cramping. Papa Rosey, for his part, relayed a crucial message when I needed it most and, in doing so, channeled the wisdom, passion, and inspiration of another individual, Dan Gable, separated greatly by time and space.[3] I was never going to quit, but Papa Rosey-cum-Gable

---

3. Gable's wisdom and inspiration were channeled to Papa Rosey and then to me, but Gable himself likely had it channeled to him by someone before him, and they to them from someone before them, ad infinitum. This is an example of how the people of the past, even the deep past, course through us.

hardened my resolve, and one can hardly have too much of that. All of this is in addition to the more ordinary yet no less valuable contributions made by Papa Rosey and Rocky as well, such as providing companionship between matches, emotional support during matches, and coaching during the timeouts of matches.

Nasty made the second most tangible contribution, as he managed to affect the outcome of a match on two separate occasions. Against Marshall Brown, I firmly believe that without Nasty's abrupt appearance, I would not have survived. Something rearranged within me upon hearing his supportive voice; I became energized again, as if his words had a direct effect on the chemistry of my mind-body. This may offer a glimpse into what Karen Barad refers to as the "eternal dance" between words and matter.[LIX] It also leads me to think that what we physically feel and believe to be our physiological state is actually, in many cases, just a convenient fiction that we choose to tell ourselves.

In the second match, versus DeHeart, Nasty's presence alone altered the course of the final points. Even though I would have likely won anyway with the lead I had built, I *was* struggling to get the last point, and pickleball leads are prone to disappear. Momentum swings are frequent and can quickly turn the tables in a match. Bullet and KO, for example, have been on both sides of these swings, with the former describing one that went in their favor:

> *"We played a 4.5 team that was in 4.0 . . . They were beating us 8-1. I was angry because they started chatting and laughing in between their serves and stuff. I said to myself, 'Okay, you're beating us 8-1, but we're really not that bad.' KO called a timeout, and all of a sudden, I played like a frickin' 5.0 player. I went on a roll. I was crushing it. We were down 8-1, and we beat them 11-8. They*

> *didn't score a single point after that. They were on the sideline, and [later] they actually took the gold medal, but they were like, 'We don't know what the hell happened.'"*

Relating this to my match versus DeHeart, there is an alternate universe in which I squandered the lead, likely to be left feeling like, "I don't know what the hell happened." Nasty, then, by momentarily distracting DeHeart, made the occurrence of such an alternate reality less of a possibility.

The rest of the supporters who were there accumulated like a snowball, as did their effect. In the qualifying, Papa Rosey and Rocky manned the sideline alone, yet as the day advanced, new personalities added their energies to our team, thus creating new entanglements and allowing for new destinies. Unsurprisingly, research has shown that support and cheering have a positive effect on performance,[LX] but even beyond that, the good vibes and well wishes helped to put me at ease between matches, and in the later matches, I gained an elevated sense of playing for someone other than myself. This was especially true versus Daescu when the intensity of my support seemed to reach a crescendo. Similar forces may have also worked *against* me in the loss to DeHeart, as it was in that match that I felt the strongest current of support for my opponent. Even relatively anonymous audience members were still intra-actors who left an imprint on the course of play, however small said imprint may be.

The last group of supporters, those who were *not* there, technically had no tangible effect but were entangled nonetheless. Going into the tournament as a big fish from two small ponds (Western Washington and Central Illinois), I was aware that my performance was of significance to a great many people. I was representing those who introduced me to pickleball (e.g., Ninja), those who helped me sustain an interest in pickleball (e.g., Beautiful), those who embraced me in a new location (e.g., Bad Boy, Big Cat, Py, The Professor), those who helped me most to refine my pickleball game (e.g., Juke, Rosey, Nasty), those who contributed to this book, and anyone else in my pickleball journey whose soul had collided with mine and who felt like they had invested a part of themselves in me. I carried these supporters like friendly ghosts, whose hopes for me hovered like an invisible halo, pushing me forward to make them proud.

The entanglement between an athlete and their supporters was made clear to me the next day on New Smyrna Beach. Around mid-afternoon, after smoking a cigar with Rocky, I hobbled along the beach alone with a jug of Pedialyte water in my hand like a canteen in a desert. It was then that I finally decided to push through the soreness and exhaustion to reply to all the messages on my phone. What I found made me sink to my knees and cry. The outpouring of congratulatory text messages from over forty contacts was overwhelming and all but affirmed that one's entanglement is sustained regardless of time and space. The support did not suddenly arise because of the tournament result (though it

A depiction of the cosmic web. This is how I envision the web of entanglements that make up an intra-action. Supporters and their effects, for example, interlink and encircle the main node that is the athlete. (Image courtesy of Wikimedia Commons.)

may have boiled over in response); it had always been present and had been absorbed over years of intra-action to take residence deep within my being. It was as much a part of me as any active bodily process, such as the respiratory and cardiovascular systems that shuttled around oxygen between points.

The final group to consider, the opponents, might be the most important piece of the puzzle. First, it must be stressed that "opponents" refers not just to the eleven tournament opponents described above but to all opponents who had contributed to the making of my pickleball being, and to an equal extent, those opponents who contributed to the making of my *opponents'* beings. I arrived at the tournament as a repository of past matches and past practices, imperceptibly shaped by each and every previous challenge,[4] as was the case, too, for my opponents in the tournament. We then performed together, aided by the lingering effects of opponents in the past, in response to the resistance of opponents in the present, and beneath the shadow cast by opponents yet to come. In this way, the tournament was no instance of finite space and time but instead a dynamic intra-action of past, present, and future.

Mentioning specific past opponents does a disservice to the hundreds of past opponents that go unmentioned, but Py and The Professor (and the treadmill) certainly helped propel me into the tournament on the right foot. Papa Rosey, the slew of opponents the two of us faced, and my early morning warm-up partner helped me build a rhythm. The opponents of my first pro tournament helped me gauge a baseline of excellence that I

---

4. The late Pat Conroy, who was a collegiate basketball player and author, touches on this sentiment in one of my favorite sports quotes: "We old athletes carry the disfigurements and markings of contests remembered only by us and no one else."[LXI]

would need to match, especially against opponents that would repeat, like Brown and DeHeart. Before that first tournament, I had never once played someone on my level, not even in practice, so this experience was quite significant. Juke, of course, also deserves a mention, as I would have been but a shell of what I was without him.

Past opponents can be entangled in ways that are not at all obvious as well. In my first pro tournament, for instance, I soared to a 5-0 lead in a match while hardly breaking a sweat. My opponent then called timeout and proceeded to have a relatively public, near-to-tears semi-breakdown in the corner of the court. A bit unnerved, I recalled a passage I had read from the famously ill-tempered tennis player John McEnroe, who describes a memorable moment with his long-term rival, Bjorn Borg:

> *"The second or third time [Borg and I] ever played, in New Orleans in early 1979, it was 5-5 in the third set, and I was getting all worked up and nutty, and Bjorn motioned me to the net. I thought, oh God, what's he going to do? Is he going to tell me I'm the biggest jerk of all time? And he just put his arm around my shoulder and said, 'It's OK, just relax.' This was at 5-5 in the third set! But he was amused by the whole thing. 'It's OK,' he told me. 'It's a great match.'"*[LXII]

With this in mind, I felt a strong yet conflicted urge to approach my opponent and comfort him. This would have been unusual and might have also jeopardized my chance to win (e.g., McEnroe calmed down, and Borg lost the match). Alas, to my great regret, I did nothing and proceeded to lose anyway. Fast forward now to the match with Daescu. During the first timeout after the match got quite testy, I felt a similar urge to show respect to my opponent and diffuse the situation somewhat by offering to tap paddles. It was similarly unusual, but this time, I did not second-guess. In this way, two opponents *before I was even born*, whom I encountered only through storytelling, intra-acted with the experience of my own opponent from months earlier and affected my behavior toward a different opponent in the tournament. If nothing else, this exposes the sheer complexity of entanglements that affect how an athlete, or anyone, behaves.

Of course, I would not have any experience worth sharing and preserving if it were not for the opponents of the tournament themselves. I am most in debt to DeHeart, whose fighting spirit and quality play forced me into the back draw and fatefully set the rest in motion. Without that defeat, it is likely that my experience would not have been nearly as transcendental. Most of my opponents, thankfully, pushed me to the brink or very near to it, thereby extracting from me the best that I had to give. I had difficulty capturing the final point on several occasions—against Lica, Sobek, DeHeart, and Daescu—which reflects the push and pull inertia of coopetition, coming out best when opponents are evenly matched. In fact, the biggest disappointments of the day were the matches that were won too easily, as those did the least to help either myself or my opponent.

The elements of nature were also "opponents," which resisted my efforts and helped co-create the matches. The wind versus Lica strongly impacted the flow of our match, as did the heat in the first match versus DeHeart. These abnormalities offered opportunities to adapt and gain a competitive advantage, though the heat mostly got the best of me. Perhaps more

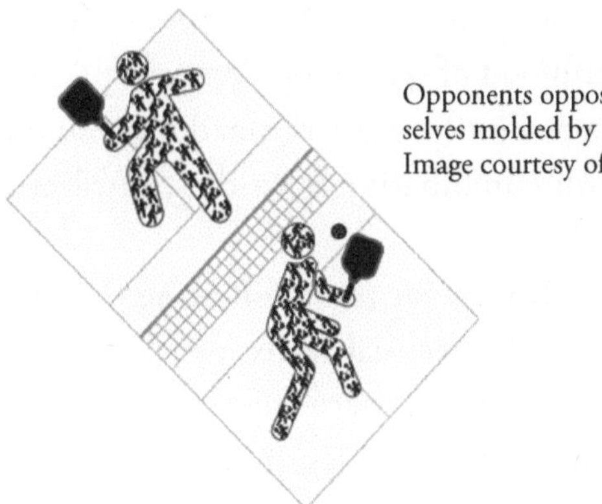

Opponents opposing each other, themselves molded by opponents' pasts. Image courtesy of Tess Manthou.

than these in terms of impact, though, was the net. In combination with the speed, angle, and spin of the ball in flight, for example, the net allowed my shot at 19-17 to dribble over versus Shick, and it is entirely possible that without this, the entire experience would not have happened. Eleven tournament matches could have easily been just one. The outcomes of intra-action in any specific case are, in this way, delicate, seeming more solid than they really are.

In conclusion, to assign anything resembling sole or majority responsibility to me for the successful outcome of "my" tournament performance would be to endow me with qualities above and beyond what I actually possess. To repeat, "I" am simply not capable of doing what "I" did. There was, instead, an impressive number of contributions from an impressive diversity of sources, including gear, grub, supporters, and opponents—past, present, and future—interwoven into what Karen Barad would call the "moments-places-matterings" of "my" tournament performance. The intra-action that made up the moments-places-matterings of the tournament led to a certain outcome, and that outcome happened to go in my favor. I, too, contributed my part, which may have nudged the likelihood of certain outcomes in particular directions, but this contribution was far from decisive and was only made possible in combination with the contributions made by others.

Additionally, dear reader, for those following the deeper argument in this book, the agential realist perspective helps illuminate the deficiencies of the zero-sum model of sports. Zero-sum assumes there are two sides, independent of each other and in competition, who are either enriched or impoverished by the result. In agential realism, zero-sum is not possible since the two sides are not independent of each other, and where there seem to be actors, there are entanglements instead. This also adds further support to a theory of coopetition in sport, in which there is constant co-creation of performance by opponents, coaches, etc., in both a competitive and cooperative sense.

13

PPA INDOOR NATIONAL CHAMPIONSHIPS

TWO WEEKS FOLLOWING the exhausting saga in Daytona Beach, I am set to play in my first PPA event, hosted south of Minneapolis. Unfortunately, Mother Nature unleashes a historic winter storm on the region in the same week, wreaking havoc on the draws. In pro mixed doubles, ten out of sixteen first-round matches are defaulted, including mine, as my mixed doubles partner, Vivian Glozman, cannot find a flight from Seattle. My preference would be to withdraw from pro doubles as well, mostly because my car is ill-equipped for a seven-hour drive in the slush and snow, but also because I have spent most of the week holed up in my apartment, with snow angels being my main source of exercise. My men's partner, Nasty, is very motivated, however, and the bad weather subsides just in time to make the trip. Plus, the PPA refuses to give refunds for poor weather without the purchase of weather insurance, even for an *indoor* tournament, so financially, I am committed.

I drive four hours the night before and spend the night on Thor's couch, then drive the remaining three hours early in the morning to arrive at the event and meet up with Nasty. The venue is large yet very chaotic and congested. The narrow walkways between courts are packed with vendors, players, and observers.[1] It is also unnecessarily loud, as the PPA blasts music from Center Court and noise seems to echo from wall to wall. I cannot even hear Nasty from across the net as we scramble from court to court, trying to warm up as matches come on and off. Altogether, I feel rushed and unsettled, and it shows in the first match. Facing the eventual silver medalists Federico Staksrud and Pablo Tellez, my nervous energy and over-arousal sink our team, falling 11-0, 11-5.

Nasty and I then find ourselves in loser's limbo, waiting for hours in a near-constant status of "next on." During this time, we spend loads of time and energy "staying warm" instead of actually competing. We do play a second match versus some 5.0 players who entered above their rank, though they perform very poorly, and it lasts less than fifteen minutes. It is five hours from the start time before we are finally on court for our third

---

1. As an observer, I imagine the venue was quite pleasurable. The venue's walkways led to a multi-storied viewing section where one could gaze over the courts from a ledge. On one of the upper floors, there was a comfy VIP lounge that was also open for the pro players to use.

match, facing off against senior pro champions Dave Weinbach and Altaf Merchant.

Little known to me in the moment, a perfect storm has slowly taken shape against me—the opposite of what happened in Daytona. I try to tell myself that I am ready to play, but there has been no rhythm to the day, and I have yet to feel comfortable. The stop-and-go hitting and staying warm has caused me to feel sluggish, like a car caught in bumper-to-bumper traffic, and the feeling is amplified by the lack of any solid breakfast or lunch. It is also early afternoon, and I feel drowsy from a lack of sleep.

Weinbach and Merchant are well known for their boisterously over-the-top competitive style, and while walking onto the court, I actually overhear a fan saying, "Altaf, I wanna see at least two hip thrusts this match!" Nasty knows them well and tries, unsuccessfully, to prepare me for their antics. Almost immediately after the match starts, I feel like I'm accosted by some humorless clowns at a twisted carnival—similar to Buddy testing jack-in-the-boxes in the movie *Elf*. In a physiological state of low arousal, I struggle to match their intensity.

Then, after a few points, Nasty calls a ball out that lands in front of me, very near the line, and Weinbach and Merchant pounce on the referee with startling ferocity, like a pack of rabid hyenas. The referee bends to their pressure and overrules the call, and from there, everything gets even worse. Waves of *C'MON's, LET'S GO's,* fist pumps, and even chest bumps wash over me, each one burying me deeper into a dark stupor, which, oddly, I cannot escape from. I feel a tremendous weight around my eyes, and everything narrows into an oppressive tunnel vision. All playfulness and fun evaporate from my being, unlike our first loss versus Staksrud and Tellez when positive vibes never left despite the lopsided score. Nasty tries his best to rally our team, but I just cannot regain any semblance of my normal self. We lose 15-4.

Embarrassed by what was easily the worst performance of my career, I quickly leave the court, essentially in fight-or-flight mode. I spend ten minutes in the locker room with a towel over my drooping head, barely taking in any sensory information. I then find a basketball and shoot hoops for thirty minutes in a gymnasium in the back of the venue. Basketball is my favorite sport, and this helps me calm down and start to process all that has happened.

Returning to the pickleball area with a sunnier disposition, I apologize to Nasty for my collapse, then watch The Flash and his partner in an entertaining match. Finally, I say my good-byes and hurry out. On the seven-hour drive home, Nasty calls me and puts on one of the most impressive performances of "friend" and "partner" I have ever known, which I love him for.

"Don't beat yourself up about it. It happens to everybody," he says.

That might be . . . but it will never again happen to me.

* * *

Pickleball, I argue, is four main things.

First, pickleball is competitive. Players try to win. There is constant push and pull. This is the foundation for all that follows.

Second, pickleball is a community. It is very social—embracing, even—despite the competition. Much of the community is enabled by features, such as the kitchen line, which allow for many types of people with different "motilities" to compete together in relative harmony.

Third, pickleball is playful. Diverse and spontaneous modes of expression are not out of place in the community. The playfulness counteracts the seriousness of competition and, in many cases, occurs along with it.

Fourth, pickleball is fun. In fact, it is so much fun that it can be *fun-dicting*. This is the natural result of mixing competitive, social, and playful components together but is also due to other basic realities of pickleball, such as being easy to play or being less physically demanding than other sports.

These four attributes contribute significantly to my broader claim that pickleball, or rather, sport, is *coopetive* and *non-zero-sum*. It is possible that pickleball is especially coopetive and especially non-zero-sum, but regardless, coopetition is not exclusive to pickleball. Instead, coopetition is a built-in feature of sport and varies in intensity depending on the sport. Though they are expressed differently, competition and cooperation always occur simultaneously in sport.

The competitive aspect of pickleball allows players to push each other and, therefore, co-create their own destinies. The sociability, playfulness, and fun of pickleball make sure that, in most cases, both the winning and losing participants receive something positive. Even in the case of highly unfavorable results, players rarely appraise their performances in zero-sum terms by tying success strictly to wins and failure strictly to losses.

The closing vignette may at first seem out-of-place, but it's included here for a couple of reasons. One of those reasons is that it subtly pokes fun at my own argument. Pickleball is supposed to be competitive, social, playful, and fun, right? Surely, the first is obvious, but how do the latter three describe the story of the PPA Indoor Championships? Indeed, the final match discussed was the least coopetive and perhaps the closest to a zero-sum session of pickleball I have been a part of. The opponents seemed to seek victory with very little of the collaborative spirit that I have come to identify so strongly with pickleball. The use of gamesmanship—the art of gaining a psychological advantage through various, often subtle acts, such as excessive celebration and noise—veers into zero-sum territory by single-mindedly gearing behavior toward a win-ning result for its own sake. And there was certainly much of this going on.

Nevertheless, to say that the match was the least coopetive I have been a part of is not to say that it wasn't coopetive; it was, only less so than usual. The opponents abided by the rules and threw up a resistance that was my/our job to match. The fact that I mostly failed to do so is my failure, to be sure, but also a collective failure, and it did them no good in the next match. Our four points also indicate some pushback, at the bare minimum. It was not a *total* failure.

Again, coopetition is not something that can be stripped away or turned off. It is expressed, to some degree, every time two or more efforts oppose each other in sport. Furthermore, I came away from the experience highly motivated to make changes to my game and refocus, which ultimately made the experience successful. My personal appraisal of the experience thus substituted for coopetition when coopetition was not as strong.

I find it poetic that the event that triggered my journey toward the concept of coopetition—the final showdown with my rival—ended with a towel draped over a dejected player's head, just as it did for me at the "end" of the journey, of sorts, in Minnesota. Of course, though the moment hurt, the wondrous fact about sport is that no matter how low one might feel after a session, an attempt was given, which is a success in its own right, and there will almost always be another opportunity to try again and wash away the old feeling with the new. Low points indicate better times to come and are simply new beginnings for an athlete's next journey. I am not sure if my rival got the opportunity of a new beginning, so I go forth with my new beginning for the two of us, in his memory.

As this book comes to a close, I feel my life's sizable debt to sport has only grown larger, and I marvel at the impact that pickleball has made on me and many others in such an unforeseen and wholly positive manner. I leave it to Wakka to express just what pickleball and sport can be, touching on much of what I have tried to argue:

"Pickleball, for me, it's important. I spend a lot of time doing it, but you know what, in a lot of ways, it really is a kind of selfish release button. It's a way I deal with a stressful job, deal with raising two teenagers, deal with life that's undoubtedly uneasy sometimes. That's just the way life is. How do I find a positive reset where, every Saturday and every Sunday, I can selfishly block out three to four hours and have something I'm really excited to do? Like, on Monday, I'm thinking, 'Holy crap, I'm gonna do better this Saturday!' So it's a release button, and it's one of the most positive ways I've found to hit that release button . . . but you know, it's a little bit more than that, [too]. If I had to call out one thing, it's a community.

I think that the older I get, having that sense of community to fall back on, to be able to open up and talk to people that aren't in my work environment . . . It's like a sounding board where I can just talk through things. That's nice. For me, pickleball is really a community, and that's the coolest thing about it. That's what keeps me coming back. I don't care if I lost or I won; I had fun. I got a chance to hit that reset button, and I have a chance the following weekend to do that again and go back to the community again. That's really what it is for me."

Everyone needs an activity that similarly enriches their life on a consistent basis. If you, dear reader, have yet to explore the game, give it a try! Or any sport, really. It may be the beginning of a new love story. Even if it's not, win or lose, the positives should outweigh the negatives. Sport is not inherently better than other things people do to find meaning in life, but I borrow from the rapper Macklemore, a fellow Seattleite, when I say that a life lived for sport is never a life wasted.

ACKNOWLEDGMENTS

THOUGH EACH LETTER in this book is the result of a tap on the keyboard from one of my fingers, single authorship is, of course, a myth, and nothing was achieved without the input of several others, all of whom I consider to be co-authors. I feel blessed, in fact, to have so many co-authors to thank.

A hearty thanks goes out to the staff at Made For Success Publishing, without whom there would be no book. Bryan Heathman and Alice Kirkwood deserve extra special recognition, as does my diligent and patient editor, Emily Waltenburg. I also wish to thank old friend Ed Sarausad, for suggesting the partnership in the first place.

Since this book was initially a Master's thesis, I am indebted to many at Illinois State University. This includes my wise and always entertaining advisor, Jim Stanlaw, and the venerable second member of my thesis committee, Wib Leonard. May they be proud of what the project has become. Other Redbird staff members who molded my thinking as it applies in this book include Gina Hunter, Thomas Burr, Bin Lizzo, and Scott Pierce. Thank you all for nourishing a young mind with wit and a smile.

I must also give a huge shout-out to the pickleball communities of Western Washington and Greater Illinois for embracing my pickleball exploits and intrusions. Of special note include Danny Long Jr., Hunter Blake, Chris Kawakita, the Rosenthal family, the Koo family, Neil Mediratta, Mary Sigmen, Michael Enright, Joaquin Flores, Ariel and Maria, and Zack AhYat. Their continued support truly means the world to me. Thank you also to current doubles partner and SoCal Hard Eights teammate, Erik Lange, for cogent advice on specific sections.

Lastly, there is nothing I do without the unwavering support of my parents, Frank and Judi, and my sister, Tess. I love you all.

APPENDIX: SPECIAL TERMS

Pickleball Terms

ATP: "Around the post." One of the most exciting and skillful shots in pickleball. If a ball is hit wide enough, it does not need to be returned above the net but can instead sail around the post mere inches above the ground.

Banger: Slang for a player who drives most balls and rarely drops or dinks. Common for tennis players.

Body Bag: Slang for a shot that (forcefully) strikes a player on the body. Called a "peg" in tennis.

Dink: A lightly tapped shot from one kitchen to the other. Dink rallies are common and can take a long time to end.

Drive: A strongly struck shot from the back end of the court.

Drop: A lightly struck shot from the back end of the court to the kitchen on the other side. Usually hit with the intention of moving forward to the kitchen. "Third shot drops" are those hit by the serving side immediately after the return.

Erne: A shot/maneuver in which a player at the kitchen line either anticipates or reacts to an opponent's shot near the sideline and then steps to the side of the kitchen and forward to volley the ball before it fully penetrates the player's side. Named after one of the original pickleball players.

Kitchen: The space between the net and the first horizontal line, called the "kitchen line." Players may not volley the ball while in the kitchen or on the kitchen line. From this rule, many of pickleball's virtues flow.

Nasty Nelson: A serve in doubles that strikes the body of the opponent not returning the serve. Named after an early pickleball player.

Pickle: Defeat in a game without a point scored. If done without once losing serve (i.e., eleven points in a row), it is called a "golden pickle."

Reset: A volley or half-volley intended to drop in the kitchen after an aggressive shot from an opponent.

Side Out: Transfer of service to the other side, i.e., both servers on a team lose their points.

Skinny Singles: One-versus-one but on only half of the court. Commonly used for training and not tournament competition, though recently some competitions have become available.

Speed Up: An aggressive shot from the kitchen following a dink or drop.

Stack: Arrangement of a doubles team so that players will only play a specific side of the court (i.e., left or right). Features a lot of switching after the return is struck, since teams must alternate who returns serve. Very common in mixed doubles or with doubles teams featuring a left-handed player. Has become the standard way of playing at higher levels.

General Racquet Sports Terms

Ace: A serve that is not returned.

Backhand: A player's stroke on their less dominant hand's side. Can be hit with one hand or two.

Forehand: A player's stroke on their more dominant hand's side. Usually hit with one hand.

Let [Court]: A ball struck that clips the top of the net to either dribble over or suddenly redirect its motion.

Lob: A shot hit very high in the air, sometimes with the intent of going over an opponent's head.

Overhead: A hard shot struck over the head after an opponent's lob. Also called a "smash."

Passing Shot: A shot intended to go by an opponent who has approached the net in singles. Often strongly struck.

Poach: An attempt to hit a volley in doubles by crossing into the partner's zone.

Return: The shot directly after the serve.

Serve: The first shot to start a point. In pickleball, serves are struck using an underhand motion with a contact point not above the waist. The ball must travel farther than the kitchen line and land into the box on the side that is not directly in front of the server. Beyond this, rules on serving tend to be in flux. As of January 1, 2023, for example, players may not spin the ball with their offhand before serving in most tournaments. There are also sometimes restrictions on how a player first drops or releases the ball to contact it.

Slice: A shot hit with underspin. Produced by hitting under the ball with a scooping or chopping motion.

Volley: A ball struck in the air before it bounces. In pickleball, volleys cannot be hit with any part of a player's body (usually feet) physically contacting the kitchen or the kitchen line, including moments after direct contact in which a player is still in a continuous motion (i.e., players cannot fall into the kitchen after contact).

Winner: A shot that lands in the court and is not touched by the opposing side.

NOTES

[I] Mehta, Pranjal, Amanda C. Jones, and Robert A. Josephs. "The Social Endocrinology of Dominance: Basal Testosterone Predicts Cortisol Changes and Behavior Following Victory and Defeat." *Journal of Personality & Social Psychology* 96, no. 6 (2008): 1078-1093.

[II] Fülöp, Márta. "Happy and Unhappy Competitors: What Makes the Difference?" *Psychological Topics* 18, no. 2 (2009): 345-367.

[III] Gauriot, Romain, and Lionel Page. "Fooled by Performance Randomness: Overrewarding Luck." *The Review of Economics and Statistics* 101, no. 4 (2019): 658–666.

[IV] Sports and Fitness Industry Association (2024). Sports, Fitness, and Leisure Activities Topline Participation Report.

[V] For the most recent press release, see "New APP Research Reveals Nearly 50 Million Adult Americans Have Played Pickleball In The Last 12 Months; Average Age Drops To 35," March 29, 2023. APP Pickleball. https://www.theapp.global/news/nearly-50-million-adult-americans-have-played-pickleball#:~:text=The%20latest%20research%20reveals%20that,are%20between%2018%20and%2024.

[VI] International Pickleball Federation. "Member Countries." Accessed August 23, 2024. https://theipf.org/countries.html.

[VII] Axelrod, Robert M., and W. D. Hamilton. *The Evolution of Cooperation*. New York: Basic Books, 1984, p.110. This is an otherwise brilliant discussion of how cooperation can evolve and thrive under certain conditions.

[VIII] For an example, see Carron, Albert V., Steven R. Bray, and Mark A. Eys. "Team Cohesion and Team Success in Sport." *Journal of Sports Sciences* 20, no. 2 (2002): 119–126. These authors measure the effect of team cohesion on team success, yet in their methodology "team success [is] operationally defined as the team's win-loss percentage" (p.120).

[IX] Bouncken, Ricarda, Johanna Gast, Sascha Kraus, and Marcel Bogers. "Coopetition: a Systematic Review, Synthesis, and Future Research Directions." *Review of Managerial Science* (2015).

[X] For an overview of the rhythm and flow of coopetition studies in business, see Gernsheimer, Oliver, Dominik K. Kanbach, and Johanna Gast. "Coopetition Research - A Systematic Literature Review on Recent Accomplishments and Trajectories." *Industrial Marketing Management* 96 (2021): 113–134.

[XI] The layout of Figure 1 is inspired by similar figures in Bengtsson, Maria, Jessica Eriksson, and Joakim Wincent. "Co-Opetition Dynamics - an Outline for Further Inquiry." *Competitiveness Review* 20, no. 2 (2010): 194–214.

[XII] 4ever3. "Darrell Waltrip on Dale Jr's Ride in the 5 Car: 'It's Coopetition.'" Web log. *SB Nation* (blog). Vox Media, April 18, 2007. https://www.sbnation.com/2007/04/darryl-waltrip-on-dale-jrs-ride-in-5.html. Though Waltrip's use of the phrase coopetition is noted in several places, this is unfortunately the only source I can find with a specific quote.

[XIII] Hehir, Jason, dir. *The Last Dance*. Episode 5, "Episode V." New York, NY: ESPN Films, 2020. The time stamp for this quote is 4:40.

[XIV] Tutko, Thomas A., and Bill Bruns. *Winning Is Everything and Other American Myths*. New York: Macmillan, 1976, p. xiii. There are also numerous other quotes in this source with strong relevance to this book's subject matter.

[XV] Rothfuss, Patrick. *The Wise Man's Fear*. New York: DAW Books, 2011, p. 420. In the scene in question, Bredon scolds the main character Kvothe for his brutish, yet temporarily successful playing of the game of *Tak*. Bredon claims Kvothe is actually getting worse and then proceeds to defeat Kvothe quickly and without effort in the next few games.

[XVI] Agassi, Andre. *Open: An Autobiography*. 1st Vintage books ed. New York: Vintage Books, 2010. Excerpt found on p. 25.

[XVII] Henry, Jules. *Culture Against Man*. New York: Random House, 1963.

[XVIII] Lutey, Tom. "Trump: We're Going to Win So Much, You're Going to Be So Sick and Tired of Winning." Billings Gazette, May 26, 2016. https://billingsgazette.com/news/state-and-regional/govt-and-politics/trump-we-re—going-to-win-so-much-you-re-going-to-be-so-sick/article_2f346f38-37e7-5711-ae 07-d1fd000f4c38.html

[XIX] Tutko and Bruns, *Winning Is Everything and Other American Myths*, 5.

[XX] Hehir, Jason, dir. *The Last Dance*. Episode 10, "Episode X." New York, NY: ESPN Films, 2020. The time stamp for this quote is 46:50.

[XXI] Henry, *Culture Against Man*.

[XXII] Preston, Cassidy, and Jessica Fraser-Thomas. "Problematizing the Pursuit of Personal Development and Performance Success: An Autoethnography of a Canadian Elite Youth Ice Hockey Coach." *The Sport Psychologist* 32, no. 2 (2018): 102–113. Quote found on p. 106.

[XXIII] Ibid., 107.

XXIV Moehringer, J. R. *The Tender Bar: A Memoir*. New York: Hachette, 2006, p. 356.

XXV Jenkins, Jedidiah. *To Shake the Sleeping Self: A Journey from Oregon to Patagonia, and a Quest for a Life with No Regret*. New York: Convergent Books, 2018, p. 156.

XXVI Wesch, Michael. *The Art of Being Human: A Textbook for Cultural Anthropology*. Manhattan, KS: New Prairie Press, 2018, p. 32.

XXVII Sports and Fitness Industry Association (2022). Sports, Fitness, and Leisure Activities Topline Participation Report.

XXVIII Ibid.

XXIX APP Pickleball, "New APP Research Reveals Nearly 50 Million Adult Americans Have Played Pickleball In The Last 12 Months; Average Age Drops To 35."

XXX Sports and Fitness Industry Association (2021). Sports, Fitness, and Leisure Activities Topline Participation Report.

XXXI Ibid.

XXXII For a closer look at the concept of motility, see Merleau-Ponty, Maurice, and Colin Smith. *Phenomenology of Perception*. Translated by Colin Smith. New York: Humanities Press, 1962.

XXXIII This definition of motility is borrowed from p. 118 of Downey, Greg. "Beneath the Horizon: The Organic Body's Role in Athletic Experience." In *Phenomenology in Anthropology: A Sense of Perspective*, edited by Kalpana Ram and Christopher Houston, 114-137. Bloomington, Indiana: Indiana University Press, 2015.

XXXIV This is a famous quip within anthropology made by the influential Clifford Geertz, found on p. 29 of Geertz, Clifford. "'From the Native's Point of View': On the Nature of Anthropological Understanding." *Bulletin of the American Academy of Arts and Sciences* 28, no. 1 (1974): 26–45.

XXXV Reilly, Rick. "Why I hate pickleball." *Washington Post*. May 8, 2023. https://www.washingtonpost.com/opinions/2023/05/08/pickleball-hate-reasons/.

XXXVI Anderson, Sally. "Bodying Forth a Room for Everybody: Inclusive Recreational Badminton in Copenhagen." In *Sport, Dance, and Embodied Identities*, edited by Noel Dyck and Eduardo P. Archetti, 23-54. Oxford: Berg, 2003. Having played both badminton and pickleball extensively, I can attest that the socio-spatial dynamic of matches (i.e. bodies in motion) is quite similar. Phrase found on p. 28.

XXXVII Wacquant, Loïc J. D. *Body & Soul: Notebooks of an Apprentice Boxer*. Oxford: Oxford University Press, 2004. Phrase found on p. 116.

XXXVIII Mastery and ego goals make up the basis of Achievement Goal Theory, first developed in Nicholls, John G. "Achievement Motivation: Conceptions of Ability, Subjective Experience, Task Choice, and Performance." *Psychological Review* 91, no. 3 (1984): 328–346. Mastery goals are those that focus on demonstrating competence in specific tasks and generally feature one's own effort and skill. In contrast, ego goals are those that focus on demonstrating a high ability and avoid demonstrating a low ability relative to others. Mastery goals are thus more desired in a coopetive framework as they allow for both sides to succeed. Research shows that it is possible to be high in both, however, and these individuals may in fact have more opportunities to pursue goals and experience success. For this last bit, see Roberts, Glyn C., Darren C. Treasure, and Maria Kavussanu. "Orthogonality of Achievement Goals and Its Relationship to Beliefs About Success and Satisfaction in Sport." *The Sport Psychologist* 10, no. 4 (1996): 398–408.

[XXXIX] Anderson, "Bodying Forth a Room for Everybody."

[XL] Goffman, Erving. The Presentation of Self in Everyday Life. Garden City, New York: Doubleday & Company, 1959. "Working consensus" is part of this classic conceptualization of interpersonal communication in sociology, and refers to how people establish a reality and cooperate together in an interaction.

[XLI] Examples of pickleball disrupting communities have become numerous, and have even led some companies to develop paddles with noise reduction technology. For one example of disrupted communities, see Solomont, E. B. "'It's Been Awkward.' Pickleball Is Pitting Neighbor Against Neighbor in Noise-Conscious Communities. Local Homeowners Associations Are Serving up Bans on the Sport, Despite Its Growing Popularity." *The Wall Street Journal. Eastern Edition*. New York, N.Y: Dow Jones & Company Inc, 2022.

[XLII] Caillois, Roger, and Meyer Barash. *Man, Play, and Games.* Translated by Meyer Barash. New York: Free Press of Glencoe, 1961. Quote found on p. 7.

[XLIII] Wacquant, *Body & Soul*, 81.

[XLIV] Agassi, *Open*, 20.

[XLV] For discussion of Gadamer's "leeway," see Nielsen, Cynthia R. "Gadamer on Play and the Play of Art." In *The Gadamerian Mind*, edited by Theodore George and Gert-Jan van der Heiden, 139-154. London: Routledge, 2021.

[XLVI] For the fun factor of pickleball among college undergraduates, see Reynolds, Erin, David N. Daum, Renee Frimming, and Katie Ehlman. "Pickleball Transcends the Generations in Southwest Indiana: A University and Area Agency on Aging Partnership Changing the Face of Aging." *Journal of Intergenerational Relationships* 14, no. 3 (2016): 242–251. For older adults, see above, and see Wray, Paige, Callahan K. Ward, Cindy Nelson, Sandra H. Sulzer, Christopher J. Dakin, Brennan J. Thompson, Matthew Vierimaa, Debasree Das Gupta, and David A. E. Bolton. "Pickleball for Inactive Mid-Life and Older Adults in Rural Utah: A Feasibility Study." *International Journal of Environmental Research and Public Health* 18, no. 16 (2021): 8374.

[XLVII] For the English version, see Huizinga, Johan. *Homo Ludens: A Study of the Play Element of Culture.* London: Routledge & Kegan Paul, 1949.

^{XLVIII} "Overturned game-winning goal AFTER trophy ceremony, a breakdown." Jomboy Media. March 22, 2022. Video, https://www.youtube.com/watch?v=hsmLpsC0Rrk&t=241s.

^{XLIX} Newman, Riley (@rileynewmanpb). "After much thought…" Instagram, May 31, 2023. https://www.instagram.com/p/Cs7dYXXgUZF/?igshid=ZWQyN2ExYTkwZQ%3D%3D.

^L In Roger Caillois's schema, "ludus," or rule-driven activity for mastery, and "paidia," or joyful improvisation and spontaneity, are two separate categories of play. Pickleball is evidence that these categories are not absolute, and an activity can, in fact, contain elements of both. For further discussion of "ludus" and "paidia," see Caillois, *Man, Play, and Games*, 27.

^{LI} Smith, Molly, Matt Denning, James Zagrodnik, and Tim Ruden. "A Comparison of Pickleball and Walking: A Pilot Study." *Medicine and Science in Sports and Exercise* 48 (2016): 93–94.

^{LII} Csikszentmihalyi, Mihaly. *Flow: The Psychology of Optimal Experience*. New York: Harper Collins, 1990. Quote found on p. 3.

^{LIII} Harwood, Chris, and Austin Swain. "The Development and Activation of Achievement Goals in Tennis: I. Understanding the Underlying Factors." *Sport Psychologist* 15, no. 3 (2001): 319-341.

^{LIV} Tutko and Bruns, *Winning Is Everything and Other American Myths*, 205.

^{LV} Agassi, *Open*, 9.

^{LVI} Barad, Karen. "Diffracting Diffraction: Cutting Together-Apart." *Parallax (Leeds, England)* 20, no. 3 (2014): 168–187. Phrase found on p. 169.

^{LVII} For the original example, see Barad, Karen. "What Flashes Up: Theological-Political-Scientific Fragments." In *Entangled Worlds: Religion, Science, and New Materialisms*, edited by Catherine Keller and Mary-Jane Rubenstein, 21-66. Fordham University Press, 2017.

^{LVIII} Sheikh, Nasreen. "A short timeline - A long journey." Nasreen Sheikh. Accessed April 20, 2023. https://www.nasreensheikh.org/.

^{LIX} Barad, Karen. *Meeting the Universe Halfway: Quantum Physics and the Entanglement of Matter and Meaning*. Durham, NC: Duke University Press, 2007.

^{LX} For an example, see Rovetta, Alessandro, and Alessandro Abate. "The Impact of Cheering on Sports Performance: Comparison of Serie A Statistics Before and During COVID-19." *Curēus (Palo Alto, CA)* 13, no. 8 (2021): e17382-.

^{LXI} Conroy, Pat. *My Losing Season*. New York: Doubleday, 2002. Quote found on p. 330.

^{LXII} McEnroe, John, and James Kaplan. *You Cannot Be Serious*. New York: G.P. Putnam's Sons, 2002. Excerpt found on p. 96.